Contents

Disclaimer 4

Introduction To Physics Engines: Concepts And Fundamentals 5
    Historical Evolution of Physics Engines in Gaming 5
    Core Principles of Physics Simulations 8
    Rigid Body Dynamics 12
    Collision Detection and Response 16
    Soft Body Physics and Deformable Objects 21
    Constraint Solvers and Joint Mechanics 26
    Integration Methods and Numerical Stability 32

Rigid Body Dynamics: Simulating Solid Objects 37
    Fundamentals of Rigid Body Kinematics 37
    Forces and Torques in Rigid Body Dynamics 41
    Energy Conservation and Work-Energy Principles 46
    Angular Momentum and Rotational Dynamics 50
    Rigid Body Equations of Motion 55
    Numerical Integration Techniques for Rigid Bodies 60
    Advanced Topics in Rigid Body Simulation 65

Soft Body Physics: Realistic Deformation And Flexibility 70
    Introduction to Soft Body Physics 70
    Mathematical Models for Soft Body Simulation 73
    Finite Element Methods in Game Development 77
    Real-Time Soft Body Collision Handling 81
    Material Properties and Deformation 85
    Optimizing Soft Body Performance for Real-Time Applications 91
    Case Studies: Implementing Soft Body Physics in Popular Games 95

Collision Detection And Response: Ensuring Realistic Interactions 100
    Fundamentals of Collision Detection Algorithms 100
    Broad-Phase vs. Narrow-Phase Collision Detection 104
    Handling Complex Interactions in Game Physics 108
    Efficient Data Structures for Collision Detection 112

    Real-Time Collision Response Techniques 116

    Optimizing Performance in Collision Handling 120

    Advanced Collision Detection Methods and Innovations 125

Fluid Dynamics: Simulating Liquids And Gases..129

    Fundamentals of Fluid Dynamics in Game Engines 129

    Navier-Stokes Equations: Governing Fluid Motion 132

    Particle-Based Methods for Fluid Simulation 136

    Grid-Based Techniques for Simulating Fluids 141

    Hybrid Approaches in Fluid Simulation 146

    Real-Time Rendering of Liquids and Gases 150

    Optimizing Fluid Simulations for Performance 155

Character Physics: Implementing Realistic Movement And Behavior 160

    Character Animation and Physics Integration 160

    Inverse Kinematics for Realistic Movement 164

    Simulating Biomechanics in Game Characters 168

    Dynamic Interaction with the Game Environment 172

    Procedural Generation of Character Behaviors 177

    Handling Character State Transitions Smoothly 181

    Physics-Based Character Controllers and AI 185

Optimization Techniques: Enhancing Performance In Physics Simulations 190

    Profiling and Benchmarking Physics Simulations 190

    Optimizing Memory Usage in Physics Engines 195

    Parallel Processing and Multithreading Techniques 198

    Adaptive Time Stepping for Performance Enhancement 203

    Level of Detail (LOD) Approaches in Physics Simulations 207

    Efficient Use of Spatial Partitioning Techniques 212

    Reducing Computational Overhead with Approximation Methods 217

intelliSoft ventures

EST 2023

Dare to Dream

Disclaimer

The information provided in this content is for educational and/or general informational purposes only. It is not intended to be a substitute for professional advice or guidance. Any reliance you place on this information is strictly at your own risk. We make no representations or warranties of any kind, express or implied, about the completeness, accuracy, reliability, suitability or availability with respect to the content for any purpose. Any action you take based on the information in this content is strictly at your own discretion. We are not liable for any losses or damages in connection with the use of this content. Always seek the advice of a qualified professional for any questions you may have regarding a specific topic.

Introduction To Physics Engines: Concepts And Fundamentals

Historical Evolution of Physics Engines in Gaming

The evolution of physics engines in gaming is a captivating journey that mirrors the broader technological advancements in computing and graphics. Understanding this historical progression provides valuable context for appreciating the sophistication of modern physics engines. This section delves into the pivotal milestones and innovations that have shaped the development of physics engines in gaming.

In the early days of video games, the concept of physics was rudimentary at best. Games like "Pong" and "Space Invaders" featured simplistic mechanics that barely scratched the surface of physical realism. The primary focus was on gameplay rather than the accurate simulation of physical phenomena. However, as gaming hardware evolved, so did the ambition of game developers.

The 1980s saw the first significant strides towards integrating physics into games. Titles such as "Asteroids" introduced basic principles of Newtonian physics, like inertia and momentum, providing players with a more immersive experience. These early implementations were limited by the processing power of the era's hardware, but they laid the groundwork for future advancements.

The 1990s marked a transformative period for physics in gaming. With the advent of more powerful consoles and personal computers, developers began experimenting with more complex physical interactions. Games like "Doom" and "Quake" showcased early forms of collision detection and response, allowing for more dynamic and engaging environments. The introduction of 3D graphics further necessitated the development of more sophisticated physics engines. This era also saw the emergence of dedicated physics libraries, such as Havok, which provided developers with tools to create more realistic physical interactions without having to build these systems from scratch.

As the new millennium approached, the demand for realism in games continued to grow. The early 2000s witnessed a significant leap in the capabilities of physics engines. Titles like "Half-Life 2" and "Grand Theft Auto III" demonstrated the potential of advanced physics simulations. "Half-Life 2" in particular was a watershed moment, utilizing the Havok physics engine to create highly interactive environments where objects behaved according to the laws of physics. This level of realism added a new dimension to gameplay, making the virtual world feel more tangible and believable.

The mid-2000s saw the rise of middleware solutions that further revolutionized game physics. Engines like PhysX, developed by NVIDIA, introduced hardware acceleration for physics calculations, significantly enhancing the performance and realism of physical simulations. This period also marked the beginning of real-time physics simulations in gaming, where complex interactions could be calculated on-the-fly, allowing for unprecedented levels of interactivity and immersion.

The past decade has seen physics engines become an integral part of game development. Modern engines like Unreal Engine and Unity come equipped with advanced physics systems that enable developers to create highly detailed and realistic worlds. The focus has shifted from merely simulating basic physical interactions to incorporating complex systems like fluid dynamics, soft body physics, and real-time destruction. These advancements have not only improved the visual fidelity of games but have also opened up new possibilities for gameplay mechanics.

In recent years, the integration of machine learning and artificial intelligence has further pushed the boundaries of what physics engines can achieve. AI-driven physics simulations can adapt and respond to player actions in ways that were previously unimaginable, creating more dynamic and responsive gaming experiences. Additionally, the rise of virtual and augmented reality has placed even greater demands on physics engines, requiring them to deliver realistic and immersive interactions in real-time.

The historical evolution of physics engines in gaming is a testament to the relentless pursuit of realism and immersion in the gaming industry. From the humble beginnings of simple 2D mechanics to the sophisticated simulations of today, physics engines have come a long way. As technology continues to advance, we can only imagine the new heights that physics engines will reach, further blurring the line between the virtual and real worlds.

In summary, the journey of physics engines in gaming reflects the broader trends in technological innovation and the ever-growing expectations of gamers. By understanding this history, we gain a deeper appreciation for the complexity and artistry involved in creating the interactive worlds that captivate and entertain millions.

Core Principles of Physics Simulations

Physics simulations form the backbone of interactive environments in modern gaming, providing players with an experience that mirrors the physical interactions of the real world. To understand how these simulations work, one must first grasp the core principles that govern them. These principles are rooted in the laws of physics and computational techniques that enable real-time execution. This section delves into the foundational concepts that underpin physics simulations in game engines, offering a comprehensive overview of their fundamental elements.

At the heart of any physics simulation are the basic laws of motion, originally formulated by Sir Isaac Newton. Newton's three laws of motion describe the relationship between a body and the forces acting upon it, as well as the body's response to those forces. The first law, often referred to as the law of inertia, states that an object will remain at rest or in uniform motion unless acted upon by an external force. This principle is crucial in simulations for maintaining the state of objects until interactions occur. The second law quantifies the effect of force on an object, stating that the force acting on an object is equal to the mass of the object multiplied by its acceleration (F = ma). This law is essential for calculating the movement of objects when forces are applied. The third law asserts that for every action, there is an equal and opposite reaction, which is key in simulating interactions between objects, such as collisions.

Beyond Newtonian mechanics, the principle of conservation is integral to physics simulations. Conservation laws, including those of energy, momentum, and angular momentum, ensure that physical properties are maintained throughout interactions. For example, in a closed system with no external forces, the total momentum before and after a collision remains constant. This principle allows simulations to accurately reflect real-world behavior, providing a sense of consistency and realism.

One of the most challenging aspects of physics simulations is collision detection and response. Collision detection involves determining when two or more objects intersect, while collision response calculates the resulting changes in motion. Efficient collision detection algorithms are crucial for real-time applications, as they must handle numerous potential interactions quickly. Techniques such as bounding volume hierarchies and spatial partitioning help optimize this process by reducing the number of checks needed. Once a collision is detected, the response phase calculates the resulting forces and adjusts the velocities and positions of the objects involved. This often involves solving complex equations to ensure that the response adheres to the principles of momentum and energy conservation.

Another fundamental concept in physics simulations is the representation of forces. Forces can be static, such as gravity, or dynamic, such as those applied by a player or an in-game event. Gravity is typically represented as a constant downward force applied to all objects, creating a sense of weight and grounding inside the game world. Dynamic forces can vary in magnitude and direction, requiring the simulation to continuously update the affected objects' states. The accurate representation and application of forces are vital for creating believable interactions and responses.

An essential component of physics simulations is the management of time. In the real world, physical processes occur continuously, but in a digital simulation, time is divided into discrete steps. This method, known as time-stepping, involves updating the state of the simulation at regular intervals. The choice of time step size is critical; too large a step can lead to inaccurate results and missed interactions, while too small a step can cause performance issues. Various techniques, such as adaptive time-stepping, adjust the step size based on the complexity of the current simulation state, balancing accuracy and performance.

Friction and restitution are also key principles in physics simulations. Friction is the resistance that objects encounter when moving against each other, which slows down motion and eventually brings objects to rest. It is typically modeled using coefficients that determine the amount of frictional force based on the materials involved. Restitution, on the other hand, describes the elasticity of collisions, determining how much kinetic energy is conserved when objects collide. A restitution coefficient of 1 indicates a perfectly elastic collision, where no kinetic energy is lost, while a coefficient of 0 represents a perfectly inelastic collision, where objects do not bounce apart.

Soft body and fluid simulations introduce additional complexity to physics engines. Soft bodies, unlike rigid bodies, can deform and change shape in response to forces. This requires advanced algorithms to simulate the internal forces and elasticity of materials. Fluid simulations, which model the behavior of liquids and gases, involve solving equations that describe fluid dynamics. These simulations are computationally intensive but add a significant layer of realism to game environments.

Finally, the integration of machine learning and artificial intelligence into physics simulations represents a cutting-edge development. These technologies can enhance the accuracy and efficiency of simulations by predicting outcomes based on vast datasets of physical interactions. AI-driven simulations can adapt to player actions in real-time, creating more responsive and immersive experiences.

In summary, the core principles of physics simulations encompass a range of fundamental concepts from classical mechanics to advanced computational techniques. Understanding these principles is crucial for creating realistic and engaging game environments. By accurately modeling motion, forces, collisions, and interactions, physics engines bring the virtual world to life, providing players with an experience that feels both tangible and dynamic. As technology continues to evolve, the sophistication and capabilities of physics simulations will undoubtedly advance, further enhancing the realism and immersion of digital worlds.

Rigid Body Dynamics

Rigid Body Dynamics is a cornerstone of physics engines, serving as the foundation for simulating the motion and interaction of solid objects in virtual environments. This section explores the essential concepts, mathematical formulations, and practical implementations that underpin rigid body dynamics in game development.

At its core, rigid body dynamics deals with objects that do not deform under applied forces. These entities maintain a consistent shape and volume, making them ideal for simulating a wide range of objects, from simple boxes and spheres to complex machinery. The primary goal of rigid body dynamics is to accurately predict the movement and interaction of these bodies based on physical principles.

One of the fundamental aspects of rigid body dynamics is the representation of an object's state. This state is typically described using position, orientation, linear velocity, and angular velocity. Position and orientation define the object's location and rotation in space, respectively. Linear velocity represents the rate of change of the object's position, while angular velocity describes the rate of change of its orientation. Together, these parameters provide a comprehensive snapshot of the object's motion at any given time.

To simulate rigid body dynamics, it is crucial to understand the forces and torques acting on an object. Forces are vector quantities that cause linear acceleration, while torques (or moments) are vector quantities that cause rotational acceleration. The relationship between forces, torques, and motion is governed by Newton's laws of motion, which provide the mathematical framework for predicting an object's behavior.

The first step in simulating rigid body dynamics is to compute the net force and net torque acting on each object. These quantities are obtained by summing all the individual forces and torques applied to the object. Common sources of forces include gravity, friction, and contact forces from collisions with other objects. Torques can arise from applied forces that do not act through the object's center of mass, as well as from rotational effects such as gyroscopic forces.

Once the net force and net torque are determined, the next step is to update the object's state using numerical integration techniques. Numerical integration involves approximating the continuous motion of the object by dividing time into small, discrete steps. At each time step, the object's position and orientation are updated based on its linear and angular velocities, which are in turn updated based on the net force and net torque.

One of the most commonly used numerical integration methods in rigid body dynamics is the Euler method. The Euler method is straightforward and computationally efficient, making it suitable for real-time applications. However, it can suffer from numerical instability and inaccuracies, especially for small time steps or stiff systems. To address these issues, more advanced integration methods, such as the Runge-Kutta method or Verlet integration, can be employed. These methods offer improved accuracy and stability at the cost of increased computational complexity.

In addition to numerical integration, rigid body dynamics simulations must also handle collisions and contacts between objects. Collision detection is the process of determining when and where two objects intersect, while collision response calculates the resulting changes in motion. Efficient collision detection algorithms are essential for real-time simulations, as they must handle numerous potential interactions quickly and accurately.

Once a collision is detected, the collision response phase begins. This phase involves computing the impulses (instantaneous changes in momentum) that resolve the collision. Impulses are applied to the colliding objects to ensure that they separate and that the principles of conservation of momentum and energy are satisfied. In some cases, additional constraints, such as joint constraints or contact constraints, may be applied to simulate more complex interactions, such as articulated bodies or frictional contacts.

Rigid body dynamics also encompasses the concept of constraints, which are conditions that restrict an object's motion. Constraints can be used to simulate joints, such as hinges or sliders, that connect multiple rigid bodies. These joints impose specific relationships between the positions and orientations of the connected bodies, allowing for the creation of complex mechanical systems. Constraints can also be used to enforce contact conditions, such as preventing interpenetration or maintaining a fixed distance between objects.

To solve the equations of motion for constrained systems, constraint solvers are employed. These solvers use techniques such as Lagrange multipliers or impulse-based methods to compute the forces and torques required to satisfy the constraints. The resulting forces and torques are then incorporated into the numerical integration process to update the state of the constrained objects.

Another important aspect of rigid body dynamics is the representation of an object's mass and inertia. Mass is a scalar quantity that measures the amount of matter in an object, while inertia is a tensor quantity that describes the object's resistance to rotational motion. The mass and inertia properties of an object determine how it responds to applied forces and torques. In simulations, these properties are often represented using mass matrices and inertia tensors, which encapsulate the distribution of mass and the rotational characteristics of the object.

In practice, rigid body dynamics simulations are implemented using a combination of mathematical models, algorithms, and data structures. These components work together to create a realistic and efficient simulation of rigid body motion. For example, spatial partitioning techniques, such as bounding volume hierarchies or grid-based methods, can be used to accelerate collision detection by reducing the number of pairwise checks. Data structures, such as linked lists or arrays, can be used to store and update the state of the simulation efficiently.

To sum up, rigid body dynamics is a fundamental aspect of physics engines that enables the realistic simulation of solid objects in virtual environments. By understanding the principles of motion, forces, torques, and constraints, developers can create simulations that accurately predict the behavior of rigid bodies. The combination of numerical integration, collision detection, and constraint solving forms the backbone of rigid body dynamics, providing the tools needed to bring virtual worlds to life. As technology continues to advance, the sophistication and capabilities of rigid body dynamics simulations will undoubtedly evolve, offering even more realistic and immersive experiences for players.

Collision Detection and Response

Collision detection and response are critical components of physics engines, responsible for ensuring that objects interact with each other in a realistic manner. This section delves into the intricate mechanisms that underpin these processes, offering a comprehensive understanding of how they contribute to the overall functionality of a game engine.

Collision detection is the first step in managing interactions between objects in a virtual environment. It involves determining whether two or more objects intersect or come into contact. This process can be computationally intensive, especially in complex scenes with numerous objects. To manage this complexity, various algorithms and data structures are employed to optimize the detection process.

One of the simplest methods for collision detection is the use of bounding volumes. Bounding volumes are simplified geometric shapes that enclose an object, such as spheres, boxes, or capsules. These shapes are chosen because they are computationally inexpensive to test for intersections. By first checking for collisions between bounding volumes, the engine can quickly eliminate objects that are not in close proximity, thereby reducing the number of detailed collision checks required.

Another approach to collision detection is the use of spatial partitioning. Spatial partitioning divides the game world into smaller regions, allowing the engine to focus collision checks on objects inside the same or neighboring regions. Common spatial partitioning techniques include grid-based partitioning, where the world is divided into a grid of uniform cells, and hierarchical partitioning, such as quadtrees or octrees, which recursively subdivide space into smaller regions. These methods help streamline the collision detection process by limiting the number of objects considered in each check.

Once potential collisions are identified, the next step is to perform precise collision detection. This involves checking for intersections between the actual geometry of the objects, rather than their bounding volumes. Techniques for precise collision detection vary depending on the complexity of the objects involved. For simple shapes, such as spheres or boxes, mathematical formulas can be used to determine intersections. For more complex shapes, such as polygons or meshes, algorithms like the Separating Axis Theorem (SAT) or Gilbert-Johnson-Keerthi (GJK) distance algorithm are employed.

The Separating Axis Theorem is particularly useful for convex shapes. It states that two convex shapes do not intersect if there exists a line (axis) along which the projections of the shapes do not overlap. By testing a finite number of potential separating axes, the engine can determine whether two convex shapes are colliding. The Gilbert-Johnson-Keerthi algorithm, on the other hand, calculates the shortest distance between two convex shapes. If the distance is zero, the shapes are in contact.

After detecting a collision, the physics engine must calculate the appropriate response. Collision response involves determining the changes in motion and position of the colliding objects to resolve the intersection and simulate realistic interactions. This process typically consists of two main phases: impulse resolution and positional correction.

Impulse resolution is the process of applying forces to the colliding objects to alter their velocities and simulate the effects of the collision. The goal is to ensure that the objects separate and that their new velocities reflect the impact. This is achieved by calculating an impulse, which is an instantaneous change in momentum, and applying it to the objects. The magnitude and direction of the impulse depend on factors such as the relative velocities of the objects, their masses, and the coefficient of restitution, which measures the elasticity of the collision.

The coefficient of restitution is a crucial parameter in collision response. It ranges from 0 to 1, with 0 representing a perfectly inelastic collision (where the objects do not rebound) and 1 representing a perfectly elastic collision (where no kinetic energy is lost). By adjusting the coefficient of restitution, the physics engine can simulate a wide range of collision behaviors, from bouncy rubber balls to sticky clay.

Positional correction is the process of adjusting the positions of the colliding objects to eliminate any remaining overlap. This step is necessary to prevent objects from getting stuck inside each other and to maintain the physical consistency of the simulation. Positional correction can be achieved using various methods, such as projecting the objects apart along the collision normal (the direction of the collision) or using constraint-based approaches that enforce non-penetration conditions.

In addition to impulse resolution and positional correction, collision response may also involve handling friction. Friction is the resistance to motion that occurs when two surfaces come into contact. It plays a vital role in collision response by affecting the tangential velocities of the objects. The physics engine typically models friction using two coefficients: static friction, which prevents objects from sliding when at rest, and dynamic friction, which resists motion when objects are already sliding. By incorporating friction into the collision response, the engine can create more realistic interactions, such as objects coming to a stop or sliding to a halt.

Handling multiple collisions and contacts is another challenge in collision response. In complex scenes, objects may experience multiple collisions simultaneously or over short time intervals. The physics engine must resolve these interactions in a consistent and stable manner to prevent erratic behavior. One approach is to use iterative solvers, which repeatedly apply collision resolution steps until the system converges to a stable state. These solvers can handle multiple contacts and constraints, ensuring that all interactions are resolved correctly.

Collision detection and response are not limited to rigid bodies. Soft bodies, such as cloth or deformable objects, and fluid simulations also require specialized techniques. For soft bodies, collision detection involves checking for intersections between the vertices or elements of the deformable mesh. Collision response must account for the elasticity and deformation of the soft body, requiring more complex algorithms to simulate realistic behavior. Fluid simulations, on the other hand, use techniques such as particle-based methods or grid-based methods to detect and respond to collisions between fluid particles or between fluids and solid objects.

To summarize, collision detection and response are fundamental aspects of physics engines that enable realistic interactions between objects in a virtual environment. By efficiently managing the detection process and accurately calculating the response, the physics engine ensures that collisions are resolved in a way that adheres to physical principles. The combination of bounding volumes, spatial partitioning, precise collision detection algorithms, and robust response techniques forms the backbone of this system. As technology advances, the methods and algorithms used for collision detection and response will continue to evolve, providing even more realistic and immersive experiences in digital worlds.

Soft Body Physics and Deformable Objects

Soft body physics represents a fascinating and complex aspect of game development, focusing on objects that can change shape and deform under various forces. Unlike rigid bodies, which maintain their form regardless of external forces, soft bodies exhibit elasticity, allowing them to stretch, compress, and bend. This capability is essential for simulating a wide range of materials and objects, from rubber balls and jelly to human tissues and clothing. Understanding the principles and methods behind soft body physics is crucial for creating realistic and immersive game environments.

At the core of soft body physics is the concept of elasticity. Elasticity refers to an object's ability to return to its original shape after being deformed by an external force. This property is characterized by two main parameters: stiffness and damping. Stiffness determines how resistant an object is to deformation, while damping describes how quickly the object returns to its original shape after the force is removed. By adjusting these parameters, developers can simulate different types of materials, from highly elastic rubber to more rigid plastics.

One common approach to modeling soft bodies is the mass-spring system. In this method, the object is represented as a network of particles connected by springs. Each particle has a mass, and the springs have properties such as stiffness and damping. When an external force is applied, the springs stretch or compress, causing the particles to move. The overall deformation of the object results from the collective movement of these particles. This model is relatively simple to implement and can produce realistic results for many types of soft bodies.

Another method for simulating soft bodies is the finite element method (FEM). FEM divides the object into a mesh of smaller elements, each with its own set of physical properties. By solving the equations of motion for each element, FEM can accurately simulate the deformation of complex shapes. This method is more computationally intensive than the mass-spring system but offers greater accuracy and flexibility. FEM is particularly useful for simulating materials with varying properties, such as heterogeneous tissues or composite materials.

In addition to elasticity, soft body physics must also account for plasticity and fracture. Plasticity refers to the permanent deformation of an object after a force exceeds a certain threshold. This behavior is common in materials such as clay or metal, which can be molded into new shapes. Fracture, on the other hand, involves the breaking or tearing of the object. Simulating these behaviors requires advanced algorithms that can detect when the material's limits are exceeded and adjust the object's geometry accordingly.

Collision detection and response are crucial components of soft body physics. Unlike rigid bodies, which have well-defined boundaries, soft bodies can change shape, making collision detection more challenging. Various techniques, such as bounding volume hierarchies and spatial hashing, can help optimize this process. Once a collision is detected, the physics engine must calculate the appropriate response, adjusting the positions and velocities of the particles or elements involved. This step ensures that the soft body interacts realistically with other objects in the environment.

One of the exciting applications of soft body physics is in character animation. Human and animal characters often have soft tissues, such as muscles and skin, that deform during movement. By simulating these tissues, developers can create more lifelike animations. For example, the muscles in a character's arm can bulge and contract as they lift an object, adding a layer of realism that static meshes cannot achieve. This technique is also used in facial animation, where the deformation of the skin and underlying muscles creates expressive and natural-looking expressions.

Cloth simulation is another area where soft body physics plays a vital role. Cloth is inherently deformable, and its behavior is influenced by factors such as gravity, wind, and collisions with other objects. Simulating cloth involves modeling the interactions between the fabric's fibers and the external forces acting on it. Techniques such as particle-based methods and FEM can be used to achieve realistic cloth simulation. This capability is essential for creating detailed and interactive clothing, flags, and other fabric-based elements in games.

Fluid dynamics is a related field that often intersects with soft body physics. Fluids, such as water and blood, can flow and deform, exhibiting both elastic and plastic behavior. Simulating fluids involves solving complex equations that describe their motion and interactions with other objects. Techniques such as smoothed particle hydrodynamics (SPH) and grid-based methods can be used to model fluid behavior. Integrating fluid dynamics with soft body physics allows for the creation of rich and dynamic environments, where characters and objects interact with water, mud, and other fluids.

The integration of soft body physics into game engines poses several challenges. One of the primary concerns is performance, as simulating deformable objects requires significant computational resources. Optimizing the algorithms and data structures used for soft body physics is essential for achieving real-time performance. Techniques such as level-of-detail (LOD) and adaptive mesh refinement can help balance accuracy and performance by simplifying the simulation for distant or less critical objects.

Another challenge is stability. Soft body simulations can be prone to numerical instability, where small errors in the calculations grow over time, leading to unrealistic behavior. Ensuring stability requires careful tuning of the simulation parameters and the use of robust numerical integration methods. Techniques such as implicit integration and constraint-based solvers can help maintain stability even in complex scenarios.

Soft body physics also presents unique opportunities for innovation. Machine learning and artificial intelligence (AI) can enhance soft body simulations by predicting and optimizing the behavior of deformable objects. For example, AI algorithms can learn from vast datasets of physical interactions to improve the accuracy and efficiency of the simulation. These advancements can lead to more responsive and realistic game environments that adapt to player actions in real-time.

In conclusion, soft body physics and deformable objects represent a critical aspect of game engine theory, enabling the simulation of a wide range of materials and interactions. By understanding the principles of elasticity, plasticity, and fracture, developers can create realistic and immersive game environments. Techniques such as mass-spring systems, finite element methods, and advanced collision detection algorithms provide the tools needed to simulate soft bodies effectively. As technology continues to advance, the capabilities of soft body physics will undoubtedly evolve, offering even more sophisticated and lifelike experiences for players.

Constraint Solvers and Joint Mechanics

In physics engines, constraint solvers and joint mechanics are pivotal components that bring realism and precision to simulations. These elements are essential for accurately modeling the interactions and limitations of objects inside a virtual environment. This section delves into the intricacies of constraint solvers and joint mechanics, providing a thorough understanding of their roles, methodologies, and applications in game development.

Constraint solvers are algorithms designed to enforce specific conditions or limitations on the movement and interaction of objects. These constraints can range from simple positional restrictions to complex relationships between multiple objects. The primary goal of a constraint solver is to ensure that the simulated objects adhere to the defined constraints while maintaining a stable and realistic simulation. This involves calculating the necessary forces and adjustments required to satisfy the constraints at each simulation step.

One of the fundamental types of constraints is the positional constraint, which restricts an object's position to a particular point or region in space. Positional constraints are often used to anchor objects to specific locations, such as attaching a character's hand to a weapon or fixing a piece of furniture to the floor. To enforce these constraints, the solver computes corrective forces that adjust the object's position, ensuring it remains inside the designated area.

Another critical type of constraint is the rotational constraint, which limits the orientation of an object. Rotational constraints are essential for simulating joints and hinges, such as those found in robotic arms or mechanical linkages. These constraints ensure that the connected objects rotate around specific axes and inside defined angular limits. By calculating the necessary torques, the solver can maintain the desired rotational relationships between the objects.

Joint mechanics is a specialized area inside constraint solvers that focuses on simulating the behavior of connected objects. Joints are the connections that allow objects to move relative to each other while adhering to certain constraints. There are various types of joints, each with unique properties and applications. Understanding the mechanics of different joints is crucial for creating realistic and functional simulations.

The simplest type of joint is the fixed joint, which rigidly connects two objects, preventing any relative movement between them. Fixed joints are used to simulate scenarios where objects must remain in a fixed position relative to each other, such as welding two metal beams together. The constraint solver ensures that the connected objects maintain their relative positions and orientations by applying the necessary forces and torques.

Hinge joints, also known as revolute joints, allow rotational movement around a single axis. These joints are commonly used in simulations of doors, wheels, and robotic arms. The hinge joint restricts movement to a specific plane, enabling the connected objects to rotate freely around the hinge axis while preventing any other types of motion. To enforce this constraint, the solver calculates the required torques to maintain the hinge's rotational behavior.

Slider joints, or prismatic joints, permit linear movement along a single axis. These joints are used in applications where objects need to slide relative to each other, such as in telescopic mechanisms or sliding doors. The slider joint restricts movement to a straight line, preventing any rotational or lateral motion. The constraint solver computes the necessary forces to ensure that the connected objects move along the defined axis.

Ball-and-socket joints, also known as spherical joints, allow rotational movement around multiple axes. These joints are used in simulations of human and animal joints, such as shoulders and hips, where a wide range of motion is required. The ball-and-socket joint enables the connected objects to rotate freely in any direction while maintaining a fixed point of connection. The solver calculates the necessary torques to preserve the joint's rotational freedom.

In addition to these basic joint types, more complex joints can be created by combining multiple constraints. For example, a universal joint, or cardan joint, allows rotational movement around two perpendicular axes. This joint is used in applications where flexible and multi-directional movement is needed, such as in drive shafts and robotic wrists. The constraint solver enforces the combined rotational constraints by calculating the required torques for each axis.

Constraint solvers utilize various mathematical techniques to enforce the defined constraints. One common approach is the use of Lagrange multipliers, which introduce additional variables to represent the constraint forces. By solving a system of equations that includes both the object's motion and the constraint forces, the solver can determine the necessary adjustments to satisfy the constraints. This method is particularly useful for handling complex and interdependent constraints.

Another approach is the impulse-based method, which calculates the instantaneous changes in velocity required to satisfy the constraints. This method is computationally efficient and well-suited for real-time applications. The impulse-based solver computes the corrective impulses at each simulation step, ensuring that the objects adhere to the constraints without introducing significant computational overhead.

Constraint solvers must also address the issue of constraint drift, which occurs when numerical errors accumulate over time, causing objects to gradually deviate from their constrained positions or orientations. To mitigate this drift, solvers often employ stabilization techniques, such as Baumgarte stabilization or constraint relaxation. These techniques introduce corrective terms that counteract the drift, ensuring that the constraints remain satisfied throughout the simulation.

Joint mechanics also play a crucial role in character animation, where skeletal structures are used to animate complex movements. Each joint in the skeleton represents a connection between bones, allowing for realistic articulation and movement. By simulating the mechanics of these joints, developers can create lifelike animations that respond naturally to external forces and interactions. For example, a character's arm can bend and rotate at the elbow and shoulder joints, enabling realistic gestures and actions.

In robotics simulations, joint mechanics are essential for modeling the behavior of robotic arms and manipulators. Each joint in the robotic arm corresponds to a motor or actuator that controls the movement of the connected segments. By accurately simulating the joint mechanics, developers can design and test robotic systems that perform precise and coordinated tasks. This capability is crucial for applications such as industrial automation, medical robotics, and autonomous vehicles.

Constraint solvers and joint mechanics are also integral to the simulation of vehicles and machinery. In these applications, joints represent the connections between various mechanical components, such as suspension systems, steering mechanisms, and drivetrain assemblies. By simulating the behavior of these joints, developers can create realistic and functional vehicle simulations that respond accurately to user inputs and environmental conditions.

The integration of constraint solvers and joint mechanics into physics engines presents several challenges. One of the primary concerns is performance, as the computational complexity of solving constraints can be significant, especially in simulations with numerous interconnected objects. Optimizing the algorithms and data structures used in constraint solvers is essential for achieving real-time performance. Techniques such as iterative solvers, parallel processing, and adaptive time-stepping can help balance accuracy and performance.

Another challenge is ensuring numerical stability, as constraint solvers must handle a wide range of scenarios and interactions without introducing instability or oscillations. Robust numerical integration methods and stabilization techniques are crucial for maintaining stability in complex simulations. Additionally, careful tuning of the solver parameters, such as constraint stiffness and damping, can help achieve stable and realistic results.

To sum up, constraint solvers and joint mechanics are fundamental components of physics engines that enable the simulation of realistic interactions and movements. By understanding the principles and methodologies behind these elements, developers can create detailed and accurate simulations that enhance the realism and immersion of virtual environments. From simple positional constraints to complex multi-axis joints, the capabilities of constraint solvers and joint mechanics are essential for bringing virtual worlds to life. As technology continues to advance, the sophistication and efficiency of these components will undoubtedly evolve, offering even more powerful tools for game development and beyond.

Integration Methods and Numerical Stability

In game development, physics engines play a pivotal role in creating immersive and realistic experiences. At the heart of these engines lies the need to accurately simulate the motion and interactions of objects inside a virtual environment. This requires the use of sophisticated mathematical techniques to integrate the equations of motion over time. The choice of integration methods and the maintenance of numerical stability are critical factors that influence the fidelity and performance of physics simulations. This section delves into the various integration methods used in physics engines and explores strategies to ensure numerical stability.

Integration methods are mathematical algorithms designed to solve differential equations, which describe the motion of objects under the influence of forces. These methods approximate the continuous changes in an object's position and velocity over discrete time steps. The accuracy and efficiency of these approximations directly impact the realism of the simulation. Several integration methods are commonly employed in physics engines, each with its own advantages and trade-offs.

One of the simplest and most widely used integration methods is the Euler method. Named after the Swiss mathematician Leonhard Euler, this method estimates the new position and velocity of an object by using its current state and the applied forces. The Euler method is computationally inexpensive, making it suitable for real-time applications. However, its simplicity comes at the cost of accuracy. The Euler method can introduce significant errors, particularly in scenarios involving large forces or rapid changes in motion. These errors can accumulate over time, leading to unrealistic behavior and numerical instability.

To address the limitations of the Euler method, the semi-implicit Euler method, also known as the symplectic Euler method, is often employed. This method improves upon the basic Euler method by first updating the object's velocity using the applied forces and then using the updated velocity to compute the new position. The semi-implicit Euler method offers better stability and accuracy, especially for systems with conservation properties, such as mechanical energy. Despite its improvements, this method can still suffer from inaccuracies in highly dynamic simulations.

Another popular integration method is the Verlet integration, named after the French physicist Loup Verlet. This method is particularly well-suited for simulations involving particles and molecular dynamics. Verlet integration calculates the new position of an object based on its current and previous positions, as well as the applied forces. By leveraging past information, Verlet integration achieves higher accuracy and stability compared to the Euler methods. It is especially effective in scenarios where forces change slowly over time. However, Verlet integration requires storing additional information, which can increase memory usage.

The leapfrog integration method, closely related to Verlet integration, is another commonly used technique. In leapfrog integration, the position and velocity of an object are updated in a staggered manner, akin to the steps of a frog leaping forward. This method offers improved stability and accuracy, particularly for systems with periodic motion, such as orbital mechanics. The leapfrog method's staggered updates help maintain the consistency between position and velocity, reducing numerical errors. However, like Verlet integration, it requires additional memory to store intermediate values.

For simulations demanding higher accuracy, the Runge-Kutta methods provide a family of integration techniques that offer greater precision at the cost of increased computational complexity. The most commonly used variant is the fourth-order Runge-Kutta method (RK4). This method calculates the new position and velocity by evaluating the forces at multiple intermediate points inside each time step. By averaging these evaluations, RK4 achieves a higher degree of accuracy and stability. However, the computational overhead of RK4 can be significant, making it less suitable for real-time applications with stringent performance requirements.

In addition to the choice of integration method, maintaining numerical stability is a crucial aspect of physics simulations. Numerical stability refers to the ability of the integration method to produce accurate and consistent results over time, even in the presence of small numerical errors. Instabilities can manifest as oscillations, divergence, or unrealistic behavior in the simulation, undermining the overall realism.

One key factor influencing numerical stability is the size of the time step used in the integration process. A smaller time step can improve accuracy and stability by reducing the approximation errors in each step. However, smaller time steps also increase the computational workload, as more steps are required to simulate a given period. Conversely, larger time steps can lead to greater errors and instabilities, particularly in scenarios with fast-moving or highly dynamic objects. Striking the right balance between time step size and computational efficiency is essential for achieving stable simulations.

Adaptive time-stepping is a technique used to dynamically adjust the size of the time step based on the simulation's requirements. In this approach, the time step is reduced in regions where the motion is highly dynamic or where forces change rapidly, and increased in regions with slower, more predictable motion. By adapting the time step to the simulation's needs, adaptive time-stepping can enhance both accuracy and stability. However, implementing adaptive time-stepping adds complexity to the integration process and requires careful tuning to avoid excessive computational overhead.

Another strategy to enhance numerical stability is the use of implicit integration methods. Unlike explicit methods, which directly compute the new state based on the current state, implicit methods involve solving a system of equations to determine the new state. Implicit methods, such as the backward Euler method, offer improved stability, particularly for stiff systems where forces change rapidly. However, solving the system of equations in implicit methods can be computationally intensive, making them less suitable for real-time applications.

Constraint stabilization is another technique used to maintain numerical stability in physics simulations. Constraints are conditions that restrict the motion of objects, such as joints or contact points. Over time, numerical errors can cause objects to drift away from their constrained positions, leading to unrealistic behavior. Constraint stabilization techniques, such as Baumgarte stabilization or projection methods, introduce corrective forces or adjustments to keep objects inside their constrained limits. These techniques help maintain the integrity of the simulation and prevent objects from violating physical constraints.

In conclusion, integration methods and numerical stability are fundamental aspects of physics engines that significantly impact the realism and performance of simulations. The choice of integration method, whether it be Euler, semi-implicit Euler, Verlet, leapfrog, or Runge-Kutta, depends on the specific requirements of the simulation and the trade-offs between accuracy and computational complexity. Maintaining numerical stability through appropriate time step selection, adaptive time-stepping, implicit methods, and constraint stabilization is essential for producing consistent and believable results. By carefully considering these factors, developers can create physics simulations that enhance the immersive experience of virtual environments. As technology continues to advance, new integration techniques and stability strategies will undoubtedly emerge, further pushing the boundaries of realism in game development.

Rigid Body Dynamics: Simulating Solid Objects

Fundamentals of Rigid Body Kinematics

Understanding the fundamentals of rigid body kinematics is essential for anyone delving into the physics of game engines. Kinematics, the study of motion without considering the forces that cause it, lays the groundwork for accurately simulating solid objects in virtual environments. This section will guide you through the core principles and mathematical frameworks that are imperative for mastering rigid body kinematics.

Firstly, we need to distinguish between different types of motion. Rigid bodies can undergo translational motion, where every point in the body moves in parallel paths, and rotational motion, where the body pivots around an axis. These two types of motion can occur independently or simultaneously, and understanding their interplay is crucial for realistic simulations.

In translational motion, the position of a rigid body is described by the coordinates of its center of mass. The velocity and acceleration of the body are the first and second derivatives of this position with respect to time, respectively. This is often represented by the equations:

$$\vec{v} = \frac{d\vec{x}}{dt}$$

$$\vec{a} = \frac{d\vec{v}}{dt}$$

where $\vec{x}$ is the position vector, $\vec{v}$ is the velocity vector, and $\vec{a}$ is the acceleration vector. These equations are fundamental in determining how an object's position changes over time under various conditions.

Rotational motion, on the other hand, involves angular displacement, angular velocity, and angular acceleration. Angular displacement (θ) describes the angle through which a point or line has been rotated in a specified sense about a specified axis. Angular velocity (ω) is the rate of change of angular displacement, and angular acceleration (α) is the rate of change of angular velocity. The relationships between these quantities can be expressed as:

$$ \omega = \frac{d\theta}{dt} $$
$$ \alpha = \frac{d\omega}{dt} $$

In the context of rigid body kinematics, it is also important to understand the concept of the moment of inertia, which is the rotational analog to mass in translational motion. The moment of inertia (I) quantifies the amount of torque needed for a desired angular acceleration about a rotational axis and depends on the distribution of the body's mass relative to that axis. The equation for rotational motion, analogous to Newton's second law for linear motion, is given by:

$$ \tau = I\alpha $$

where τ is the torque applied to the object. This equation helps in predicting how an object will respond to rotational forces.

Combining translational and rotational motion, the overall state of a rigid body in motion can be described using a combination of linear and angular quantities. For practical purposes, this involves the use of vectors and matrices to handle the complex interplay between these types of motion. For example, the velocity of a point on a rotating body can be expressed as:

$$\vec{v}_{\text{point}} = \vec{v}_{\text{cm}} + \vec{\omega} \times \vec{r}$$

where $\vec{v}_{\text{cm}}$ is the velocity of the center of mass, $\vec{\omega}$ is the angular velocity, and $\vec{r}$ is the position vector of the point relative to the center of mass.

To implement these concepts in a game engine, one must utilize numerical methods to solve the differential equations governing motion. Techniques such as the Euler method, Runge-Kutta methods, and Verlet integration are commonly used to approximate the solutions of these equations over discrete time steps. Each method has its advantages and trade-offs in terms of accuracy, stability, and computational efficiency.

Moreover, quaternions are often employed in game engines for representing rotations. Unlike Euler angles, quaternions avoid gimbal lock and provide a more robust way to interpolate between orientations. A quaternion is a four-dimensional complex number that can represent any rotation in three-dimensional space. The use of quaternions for rotation calculations simplifies the process of combining multiple rotations and ensures smoother transitions.

In summary, the fundamentals of rigid body kinematics encompass the study of both translational and rotational motion, the mathematical relationships that describe these motions, and the methods for implementing them in a game engine. By mastering these principles, one can create simulations that accurately reflect the physical behaviors of solid objects, thereby enhancing the realism and interactivity of virtual environments. Understanding and applying these concepts is a critical step in the journey to becoming an adept game engine developer.

Forces and Torques in Rigid Body Dynamics

In game engine physics, the accurate simulation of solid objects hinges on a thorough understanding of forces and torques. These fundamental concepts are instrumental in predicting and controlling the movement and interaction of objects inside a virtual environment. This section delves into the intricacies of forces and torques, elucidating their roles and applications in rigid body dynamics.

Forces, in essence, are interactions that change the motion of an object. In the context of rigid body dynamics, forces can be categorized into several types, including gravitational, normal, frictional, and applied forces. Gravitational force, for instance, is a universal attraction exerted by the Earth on all objects, pulling them towards its center. This force is represented mathematically by Newton's law of universal gravitation:

$$ F_g = m \cdot g $$

where $ F_g $ is the gravitational force, $ m $ is the mass of the object, and $ g $ is the acceleration due to gravity, approximately $ 9.81 \, m/s^2 $ on the surface of the Earth.

Normal force is the perpendicular contact force exerted by a surface on an object in contact with it. It acts in opposition to the gravitational force, preventing the object from accelerating through the surface. Frictional force, on the other hand, resists the relative motion of two surfaces in contact. It is a function of the normal force and the coefficient of friction between the surfaces, expressed as:

\[F_f = \mu \cdot F_n \]

where \(F_f \) is the frictional force, \(\mu \) is the coefficient of friction, and \(F_n \) is the normal force.

Applied forces are those exerted on objects by external agents, such as a player pushing a block in a game. These forces can be directional and vary in magnitude, influencing the object's motion according to Newton's second law of motion:

\[F = m \cdot a \]

where \(F \) is the net force acting on the object, \(m \) is its mass, and \(a \) is the resulting acceleration.

Torques, or moments of force, are rotational analogs to linear forces. They induce rotational motion around an axis and are a product of the force applied and the distance from the axis of rotation, known as the lever arm. The mathematical representation of torque is given by:

\[\tau = r \cdot F \cdot \sin(\theta) \]

where \(\tau \) is the torque, \(r \) is the lever arm, \(F \) is the applied force, and \(\theta \) is the angle between the force vector and the lever arm. The direction of the torque vector is determined by the right-hand rule, which states that if the fingers of the right hand curl in the direction of the force, the thumb points in the direction of the torque.

In rigid body dynamics, it is crucial to consider both the net force and the net torque acting on an object. The net force influences the linear acceleration of the object's center of mass, while the net torque affects its angular acceleration. These relationships are encapsulated in the equations of motion for translation and rotation:

$$ F_{net} = m \cdot a $$

$$ \tau_{net} = I \cdot \alpha $$

where F_{net} is the net force, τ_{net} is the net torque, I is the moment of inertia, and α is the angular acceleration. The moment of inertia is a measure of an object's resistance to changes in its rotational motion, dependent on its mass distribution relative to the axis of rotation.

The interplay between forces and torques becomes particularly significant when simulating collisions and interactions between objects. During a collision, impulses are exchanged, altering the linear and angular velocities of the objects involved. An impulse is the integral of force over the time interval of the collision, and it results in a change in momentum:

$$ J = \Delta p = F \cdot \Delta t $$

where J is the impulse, Δp is the change in momentum, F is the average force during the collision, and Δt is the duration of the collision. For rotational motion, the angular impulse is given by:

$$ J_{\tau} = \Delta L = \tau \cdot \Delta t $$

where J_{τ} is the angular impulse, ΔL is the change in angular momentum, τ is the average torque, and Δt is the duration of the torque application.

In practical applications inside game engines, numerical integration methods are employed to update the state of rigid bodies over discrete time steps. Techniques such as the Euler method, symplectic Euler, and the Runge-Kutta methods are commonly used to approximate the solutions to the equations of motion. These methods iteratively compute the positions, velocities, and orientations of objects, ensuring that the simulation remains stable and accurate over time.

Moreover, constraints and joints are often implemented to control the motion of rigid bodies in a game environment. Constraints restrict the degrees of freedom of an object, enforcing specific conditions on its motion. Joints, such as hinge joints, slider joints, and ball-and-socket joints, connect two or more rigid bodies, allowing for complex interactions and articulated structures. The forces and torques generated by these constraints and joints are calculated using constraint solvers, which ensure that the imposed conditions are satisfied at each time step.

To sum it all up, the study of forces and torques is fundamental to the simulation of rigid body dynamics in game engines. By understanding the principles governing these interactions, developers can create realistic and engaging virtual environments. The accurate modeling of forces and torques not only enhances the physical realism of the simulation but also contributes to the overall immersion and interactivity of the game.

Through the application of these concepts, one can achieve a deeper understanding of the mechanics underlying rigid body dynamics and their implementation in game development.

Energy Conservation and Work-Energy Principles

In simulating solid objects inside game engines, the principles of energy conservation and work-energy play a pivotal role. These concepts are fundamental to ensuring realistic and physically accurate behavior of objects. By understanding how energy transforms and is conserved, developers can create more immersive and believable simulations.

The conservation of energy principle states that the total energy inside a closed system remains constant over time. This principle is paramount in physics and has significant implications for game engine dynamics. Energy can exist in various forms, including kinetic energy, potential energy, and thermal energy. When simulating rigid bodies, the focus is primarily on kinetic and potential energy.

Kinetic energy is the energy of motion. For a rigid body, it is derived from both translational and rotational movements. The translational kinetic energy is given by the equation:

$$ KE_{\text{trans}} = \frac{1}{2} m v^2 $$

where m is the mass of the object and v is its velocity. This equation highlights that the kinetic energy increases with the square of the velocity, indicating that faster-moving objects possess significantly more energy.

Rotational kinetic energy, on the other hand, is associated with the rotation of a rigid body around its center of mass. It is represented by:

\[KE_{\text{rot}} = \frac{1}{2} I \omega^2 \]

where \(I \) is the moment of inertia and \(\omega \) is the angular velocity. The moment of inertia depends on the mass distribution relative to the axis of rotation, and it quantifies the resistance to rotational motion.

Potential energy is the stored energy of position. In the context of rigid body dynamics, gravitational potential energy is the most relevant. It is calculated using the formula:

\[PE_{\text{grav}} = mgh \]

where \(g \) is the acceleration due to gravity and \(h \) is the height of the object above a reference point. This form of energy is crucial for simulating scenarios where objects are elevated and can fall under the influence of gravity.

To ensure the conservation of energy inside a game engine, it is essential to account for the transformation between kinetic and potential energy. For instance, as an object falls, its potential energy decreases while its kinetic energy increases, maintaining the total energy constant. This transformation is governed by the work-energy principle, which states that the work done on an object is equal to the change in its kinetic energy.

Work is defined as the product of the force applied to an object and the displacement in the direction of the force. Mathematically, it is expressed as:

\[W = \vec{F} \cdot \vec{d} \]

where $\vec{F}$ is the force vector and $\vec{d}$ is the displacement vector. Work can be positive or negative, depending on whether the force acts in the direction of the displacement or opposite to it.

When an external force does work on a rigid body, it changes the body's kinetic energy. This relationship is captured by the work-energy theorem:

$$W = \Delta KE$$

where ΔKE is the change in kinetic energy. If the work done is positive, the kinetic energy increases; if negative, it decreases.

Incorporating these principles into game engine simulations involves careful numerical integration to ensure energy consistency over time. Various methods, such as the Verlet integration and symplectic Euler method, are utilized to update the positions and velocities of objects while preserving energy conservation. These techniques help mitigate numerical errors that can accumulate and lead to unrealistic behavior.

Additionally, energy dissipation mechanisms, such as friction and air resistance, play a crucial role in maintaining realism. These forces convert kinetic energy into thermal energy, gradually reducing the motion of objects. Properly modeling these dissipative forces ensures that objects come to rest naturally, rather than perpetually moving, which would violate energy conservation.

In summary, the principles of energy conservation and work-energy are foundational to simulating solid objects in game engines. By understanding and applying these concepts, developers can create simulations that accurately reflect the physical behaviors of rigid bodies. The transformation and conservation of energy provide a framework for predicting and controlling the motion of objects, enhancing the realism and interactivity of virtual environments. Through meticulous implementation of these principles, one can achieve a deeper appreciation and mastery of rigid body dynamics in game development.

Angular Momentum and Rotational Dynamics

Simulating the rotational behavior of solid objects inside game engines requires a thorough grasp of angular momentum and rotational dynamics. These concepts are vital for creating realistic and engaging virtual environments, as they govern how objects spin, rotate, and respond to applied forces. This section delves into the intricacies of angular momentum and rotational dynamics, exploring their mathematical foundations, physical interpretations, and practical applications in game development.

Angular momentum, a cornerstone of rotational dynamics, is a measure of an object's rotational motion. It is analogous to linear momentum in translational motion but applies to rotation around an axis. The angular momentum of a rigid body depends on its moment of inertia and angular velocity. Mathematically, angular momentum ($\vec{L}$) is defined as:

$$\vec{L} = I \vec{\omega}$$

where I is the moment of inertia and $\vec{\omega}$ is the angular velocity vector. The moment of inertia quantifies the distribution of an object's mass relative to the axis of rotation, while angular velocity describes the rate of rotation.

Understanding the moment of inertia is crucial for simulating rotational dynamics accurately. The moment of inertia depends on both the mass of the object and its geometry. For example, a solid sphere and a hollow cylinder of the same mass will have different moments of inertia due to their distinct mass distributions. The moment of inertia for various shapes can be calculated using standard formulas, such as:

- For a solid sphere of radius r:

$$I = \frac{2}{5} m r^2$$

- For a solid cylinder of radius r and height h:

$$I = \frac{1}{2} m r^2$$

- For a thin rod of length l rotating about its center:

$$I = \frac{1}{12} m l^2$$

These formulas highlight how the geometry of an object influences its rotational properties. In game engines, precomputed moments of inertia for common shapes are often used to optimize performance and simplify calculations.

Angular momentum is conserved in the absence of external torques. This principle, known as the conservation of angular momentum, states that the total angular momentum of a closed system remains constant over time. This conservation law has profound implications for the behavior of rotating objects. For instance, when a figure skater pulls in their arms during a spin, their moment of inertia decreases, causing their angular velocity to increase to conserve angular momentum. This effect is essential for simulating realistic rotational behaviors in games.

To change an object's angular momentum, a torque must be applied. Torque is the rotational equivalent of force and causes changes in angular velocity. The relationship between torque ($\vec{\tau}$) and angular momentum is given by:

$$\vec{\tau} = \frac{d\vec{L}}{dt}$$

where $\frac{d\vec{L}}{dt}$ is the time derivative of angular momentum. This equation indicates that the rate of change of angular momentum is equal to the applied torque. In practical terms, applying a torque to an object will cause it to accelerate rotationally, altering its angular velocity.

In game engines, simulating torque involves calculating the effect of forces applied at specific points on an object. The torque produced by a force ($\vec{F}$) applied at a point with position vector $\vec{r}$ relative to the axis of rotation is given by:

$$\vec{\tau} = \vec{r} \times \vec{F}$$

where $\times$ denotes the cross product. The direction of the torque vector is perpendicular to both $\vec{r}$ and $\vec{F}$, following the right-hand rule. This calculation is fundamental for simulating realistic interactions, such as a character pushing a door or a ball rolling down a slope.

Rotational dynamics also involve rotational kinetic energy, which is the energy associated with an object's rotation. Rotational kinetic energy (KE_{rot}) is given by:

$$KE_{\text{rot}} = \frac{1}{2} I \omega^2$$

This equation illustrates that rotational kinetic energy depends on both the moment of inertia and the square of the angular velocity. In game engines, conserving energy during rotational interactions is essential for maintaining physical realism. For example, when two objects collide and exchange rotational energy, the total energy before and after the collision should remain consistent, accounting for any energy losses due to friction or other dissipative forces.

Implementing rotational dynamics in game engines requires sophisticated numerical methods to solve the equations of motion. Techniques such as the Runge-Kutta method and quaternion-based rotations are commonly used to update the orientation and angular velocity of objects over discrete time steps. Quaternions, in particular, provide a robust way to represent rotations without suffering from the gimbal lock issue inherent in Euler angles. A quaternion is a four-dimensional complex number that can represent any rotation in three-dimensional space, making it ideal for smooth and continuous rotations in games.

Moreover, constraints and joints play a pivotal role in controlling rotational dynamics inside game environments. Constraints restrict the degrees of freedom of an object's motion, ensuring that it adheres to specific conditions. Joints, such as hinge joints, slider joints, and ball-and-socket joints, connect multiple rigid bodies, allowing for complex interactions and articulated structures. The forces and torques generated by these constraints and joints are calculated using advanced algorithms, ensuring that the imposed conditions are satisfied at each time step.

One common application of angular momentum and rotational dynamics in games is the simulation of spinning objects, such as wheels, gears, and propellers. These objects exhibit rotational motion that must be accurately modeled to enhance the player's experience. For instance, a car's wheels must rotate realistically as it accelerates, decelerates, and turns. By applying the principles of angular momentum and torque, developers can create lifelike simulations of such objects, contributing to the overall immersion of the game.

In summary, angular momentum and rotational dynamics are fundamental components of simulating solid objects in game engines. Understanding the mathematical relationships between angular momentum, torque, and rotational motion is crucial for creating realistic and engaging virtual environments. By leveraging these principles, developers can accurately model the rotational behaviors of objects, ensuring that they respond appropriately to applied forces and torques. Through the careful application of numerical methods and the implementation of constraints and joints, one can achieve a deeper understanding of rotational dynamics and their critical role in game development.

Rigid Body Equations of Motion

The simulation of solid objects in game engines is a complex task that requires a fundamental understanding of the equations of motion governing rigid bodies. This section explores the mathematical formulations and principles that underpin the movement and interaction of solid objects in a virtual environment. By delving into these equations, developers can create more accurate and realistic simulations, enhancing the overall gaming experience.

Rigid body dynamics is an area of physics that deals with the motion of solid objects that do not deform under the influence of forces. These objects are characterized by having a fixed shape and size, which simplifies the mathematical modeling of their motion. The behavior of rigid bodies is described by a set of equations that account for both translational and rotational movements. These equations are derived from Newton's laws of motion and provide a comprehensive framework for predicting the motion of rigid bodies.

The translational motion of a rigid body is described by Newton's second law, which states that the acceleration of an object is directly proportional to the net force acting on it and inversely proportional to its mass. This relationship is expressed mathematically as:

$$\vec{a} = \frac{\vec{F}_{\text{net}}}{m}$$

where $\vec{a}$ is the acceleration, $\vec{F}_{\text{net}}$ is the net force acting on the body, and m is the mass of the body. The net force is the vector sum of all external forces acting on the body, and it determines the rate of change of the body's velocity. By integrating this equation over time, we can compute the velocity and position of the body at any given moment.

In addition to translational motion, rigid bodies also undergo rotational motion. The rotational analog of Newton's second law is given by the equation:

$$\vec{\alpha} = \frac{\vec{\tau}_{\text{net}}}{I}$$

where $\vec{\alpha}$ is the angular acceleration, $\vec{\tau}_{\text{net}}$ is the net torque acting on the body, and I is the moment of inertia. The moment of inertia is a measure of an object's resistance to changes in its rotational motion and depends on the mass distribution relative to the axis of rotation. The net torque is the vector sum of all external torques acting on the body, and it determines the rate of change of the body's angular velocity.

The equations of motion for a rigid body can be further refined by considering the forces and torques acting on the body in more detail. For example, the gravitational force acting on a body is given by:

$$\vec{F}_g = m \vec{g}$$

where $\vec{g}$ is the acceleration due to gravity. The normal force, which is the perpendicular contact force exerted by a surface on the body, can be represented as:

$$\vec{F}_n = - m \vec{g}$$

Frictional forces, which resist the relative motion of two surfaces in contact, can be modeled using the equation:

$$\vec{F}_f = \mu \vec{F}_n$$

where μ is the coefficient of friction. Applied forces, such as those exerted by a player on an object, can be represented by:

$$\vec{F}_{\text{applied}} = m \vec{a}_{\text{applied}}$$

where $\vec{a}_{\text{applied}}$ is the applied acceleration.

The net force acting on a rigid body is the sum of all these forces:

$$\vec{F}_{\text{net}} = \vec{F}_g + \vec{F}_n + \vec{F}_f + \vec{F}_{\text{applied}}$$

Similarly, the net torque acting on a rigid body is the sum of all torques:

$$\vec{\tau}_{\text{net}} = \vec{\tau}_g + \vec{\tau}_n + \vec{\tau}_f + \vec{\tau}_{\text{applied}}$$

where $\vec{\tau}_g$, $\vec{\tau}_n$, $\vec{\tau}_f$, and $\vec{\tau}_{\text{applied}}$ are the torques due to gravitational, normal, frictional, and applied forces, respectively.

To simulate the motion of a rigid body in a game engine, numerical integration methods are used to solve these equations over discrete time steps. One common method is the Euler integration, which updates the position and velocity of the body using the equations:

$$\vec{v}(t + \Delta t) = \vec{v}(t) + \vec{a}(t) \Delta t$$

$$\vec{r}(t + \Delta t) = \vec{r}(t) + \vec{v}(t) \Delta t$$

where $\vec{v}(t)$ and $\vec{r}(t)$ are the velocity and position of the body at time t, and Δt is the time step. While simple and easy to implement, the Euler method can be prone to numerical inaccuracies and instability, especially for stiff systems.

More advanced integration methods, such as the Runge-Kutta and Verlet methods, offer improved accuracy and stability. The Runge-Kutta method, for instance, calculates intermediate steps inside each time step to provide a more accurate approximation of the body's motion. The Verlet method, on the other hand, uses both the current and previous positions to compute the next position, reducing numerical errors.

In addition to numerical integration, constraints and joints are often used to control the motion of rigid bodies in a game environment. Constraints restrict the degrees of freedom of a body, ensuring that it adheres to specific conditions. For example, a ball rolling on a surface is constrained to move along the surface without penetrating it. Joints, such as hinge joints and ball-and-socket joints, connect multiple rigid bodies, allowing for complex interactions and articulated structures. The forces and torques generated by these constraints and joints are calculated using constraint solvers, which ensure that the imposed conditions are satisfied at each time step.

The accurate simulation of rigid body dynamics also requires consideration of collision detection and response. When two rigid bodies collide, impulses are exchanged, altering their velocities and angular velocities. Collision detection algorithms identify when and where collisions occur, while collision response algorithms compute the resulting changes in motion. These algorithms must account for factors such as the relative velocities and masses of the colliding bodies, as well as the coefficients of restitution and friction.

To sum it all up, the equations of motion for rigid bodies provide a comprehensive framework for simulating the behavior of solid objects in game engines. By understanding and applying these equations, developers can create realistic and engaging virtual environments. The accurate modeling of forces, torques, and constraints is essential for achieving physical realism, while numerical integration methods and collision algorithms ensure stability and accuracy over time. Through meticulous implementation of these principles, one can achieve a deeper understanding of rigid body dynamics and their critical role in game development.

Numerical Integration Techniques for Rigid Bodies

In the context of simulating rigid bodies inside game engines, numerical integration techniques are indispensable. These methods allow developers to approximate the continuous motion of objects through discrete time steps, ensuring accurate and realistic simulations. This section delves into various numerical integration techniques employed in rigid body dynamics, highlighting their strengths, limitations, and practical applications.

Numerical integration is essential because it bridges the gap between theoretical physics and computational implementation. The equations of motion governing rigid bodies are typically expressed in differential form, which describes how quantities such as position and velocity change over time. However, computers operate in discrete intervals, necessitating the use of numerical methods to approximate these continuous changes.

One of the simplest and most intuitive numerical integration techniques is the Euler method. This approach updates an object's position and velocity based on its current state and the forces acting upon it. The Euler method is expressed mathematically as:

$$v(t + \Delta t) = v(t) + a(t) * \Delta t$$
$$r(t + \Delta t) = r(t) + v(t) * \Delta t$$

where v represents velocity, r denotes position, a stands for acceleration, and Δt is the time step. While the Euler method is straightforward to implement, it has limitations. It can suffer from numerical instability and inaccuracy, particularly when dealing with stiff systems or large time steps. Despite these drawbacks, the Euler method remains a valuable tool for quick prototyping and simple simulations.

To address the limitations of the Euler method, more sophisticated techniques such as the Midpoint method and the Runge-Kutta methods have been developed. The Midpoint method, also known as the modified Euler method, improves upon the basic Euler approach by calculating the state at the midpoint of the time step. This intermediate state is then used to update the final position and velocity. The Midpoint method is expressed as:

$k1 = a(t) * \Delta t$

$v\_mid = v(t) + k1 / 2$

$r\_mid = r(t) + v(t) * \Delta t / 2$

$k2 = a(t + \Delta t / 2) * \Delta t$

$v(t + \Delta t) = v(t) + k2$

$r(t + \Delta t) = r(t) + v\_mid * \Delta t$

This technique offers improved accuracy over the basic Euler method by considering the acceleration at the midpoint, reducing the error introduced in each time step.

Among the most widely used numerical integration techniques in rigid body dynamics is the Runge-Kutta method, particularly the fourth-order Runge-Kutta (RK4) method. The RK4 method provides a high degree of accuracy by evaluating the derivatives at multiple points inside the time step and combining them to obtain the final state. The RK4 method is expressed as:

$k1 = a(t) * \Delta t$

$k2 = a(t + \Delta t / 2) * \Delta t$

$k3 = a(t + \Delta t / 2) * \Delta t$

$k4 = a(t + \Delta t) * \Delta t$

$v(t + \Delta t) = v(t) + (k1 + 2*k2 + 2*k3 + k4) / 6$

$r(t + \Delta t) = r(t) + (k1 + 2*k2 + 2*k3 + k4) / 6$

The RK4 method is highly regarded for its balance between computational efficiency and accuracy, making it a popular choice for simulating complex systems where precision is paramount.

Another powerful technique for numerical integration in rigid body dynamics is the Verlet method. The Verlet method is particularly well-suited for systems where conservation of energy is crucial, such as in celestial mechanics and molecular dynamics. The Verlet method updates positions based on both the current and previous states, reducing numerical errors. It is expressed as:

$r(t + \Delta t) = 2 * r(t) - r(t - \Delta t) + a(t) * \Delta t^2$

The Verlet method's primary advantage is its ability to maintain stability and accuracy over long simulations, even with relatively large time steps. However, it requires storing the previous state, which can increase memory usage.

A variation of the Verlet method, known as the Velocity Verlet method, addresses the need to directly update velocities. It is expressed as:

$$r(t + \Delta t) = r(t) + v(t) * \Delta t + 0.5 * a(t) * \Delta t^2$$

$$v(t + \Delta t) = v(t) + 0.5 * (a(t) + a(t + \Delta t)) * \Delta t$$

The Velocity Verlet method combines the stability of the original Verlet method with the ability to update velocities directly, making it a versatile choice for many simulations.

In addition to these techniques, implicit integration methods are also employed in rigid body dynamics, particularly for stiff systems where explicit methods may fail. Implicit methods, such as the Backward Euler method, involve solving equations that include the unknown future state, requiring iterative solvers. While computationally more intensive, implicit methods offer superior stability for stiff problems. The Backward Euler method is expressed as:

$$v(t + \Delta t) = v(t) + a(t + \Delta t) * \Delta t$$

$$r(t + \Delta t) = r(t) + v(t + \Delta t) * \Delta t$$

Implicit methods are particularly useful in scenarios where large forces or rapid changes in motion occur, ensuring the stability and accuracy of the simulation.

In practical applications, game engines often employ a combination of these numerical integration techniques to balance performance and accuracy. For example, simpler methods like the Euler or Midpoint methods may be used for non-critical background objects, while more accurate methods like RK4 or implicit methods are reserved for key interactive elements.

Furthermore, adaptive time-stepping techniques can be employed to dynamically adjust the time step based on the simulation's requirements. By reducing the time step during periods of rapid change and increasing it during stable periods, adaptive time-stepping ensures both accuracy and computational efficiency.

To sum it all up, numerical integration techniques are fundamental to simulating rigid bodies in game engines. From the basic Euler method to advanced techniques like the Runge-Kutta and Verlet methods, each approach offers unique advantages and trade-offs. By understanding and applying these techniques, developers can create realistic and engaging simulations, enhancing the overall gaming experience. Through careful selection and implementation of numerical integration methods, one can achieve a deeper appreciation and mastery of rigid body dynamics in game development.

Advanced Topics in Rigid Body Simulation

In the realm of game development, simulating the behavior of solid objects with high fidelity is paramount for creating immersive and interactive virtual worlds. While basic rigid body dynamics provide a solid foundation, delving into advanced topics allows for even more realistic and complex simulations. This section explores some of the sophisticated techniques and considerations that elevate rigid body simulation to the next level.

One of the key advanced topics in rigid body simulation is the handling of articulated structures. These structures consist of multiple interconnected rigid bodies, such as a character's skeleton or a mechanical arm. Each segment of the structure is treated as a separate rigid body, but their movements are constrained by joints. These joints can be of various types, including revolute, prismatic, and spherical, each allowing different degrees of freedom. Properly simulating articulated structures requires solving the constraints imposed by the joints, ensuring that the segments move in a coordinated manner. This often involves using constraint solvers, which iteratively adjust the positions and orientations of the rigid bodies to satisfy the joint constraints.

Another advanced topic is the simulation of deformable bodies. Unlike rigid bodies, deformable bodies can change shape in response to forces. This is particularly important for simulating soft materials, such as cloth, jelly, or human tissue. Deformable body simulation typically involves representing the body as a mesh of interconnected particles or finite elements. The forces acting on these particles or elements are computed, and their positions are updated accordingly. This requires solving complex equations that account for both the internal forces inside the body and the external forces acting upon it. Advanced techniques, such as mass-spring systems, finite element methods, and position-based dynamics, are often employed to achieve realistic deformation effects.

Collision detection and response are also crucial components of advanced rigid body simulation. In complex scenes with many interacting objects, efficiently detecting and resolving collisions becomes a significant challenge. Broad-phase collision detection algorithms, such as spatial partitioning and bounding volume hierarchies, are used to quickly identify potential collisions between objects. Once potential collisions are detected, narrow-phase algorithms, such as the Gilbert-Johnson-Keerthi (GJK) algorithm and the Minkowski difference approach, are used to precisely determine the points of contact and compute the collision response. Handling collisions robustly involves not only resolving the interpenetration of objects but also accounting for friction, restitution, and other physical properties that influence the outcome of collisions.

In addition to handling collisions, managing contact forces is another advanced topic in rigid body simulation. When rigid bodies are in contact, they exert forces on each other to prevent interpenetration. These contact forces can be modeled using various techniques, such as penalty methods, constraint-based methods, and impulse-based methods. Penalty methods apply forces proportional to the amount of interpenetration, acting as a spring-like force to push the bodies apart. Constraint-based methods, on the other hand, treat contact as a constraint that must be satisfied, using constraint solvers to compute the necessary forces. Impulse-based methods apply instantaneous impulses to adjust the velocities of the bodies, ensuring that they separate appropriately. Each of these methods has its advantages and trade-offs, and the choice of method depends on the specific requirements of the simulation.

Another important aspect of advanced rigid body simulation is the incorporation of external forces and environmental effects. Rigid bodies in a game world are often subjected to forces such as gravity, wind, and buoyancy. Accurately modeling these forces requires understanding their physical properties and how they interact with the rigid bodies. For example, buoyancy forces depend on the volume of the submerged part of the body and the density of the fluid. Wind forces are influenced by the shape and orientation of the body relative to the wind direction. Incorporating these external forces into the simulation adds an extra layer of realism, making the virtual world more believable and dynamic.

The simulation of fluids and gases is another advanced topic that intersects with rigid body dynamics. Fluids, such as water and air, interact with rigid bodies in complex ways, influencing their motion and behavior. Simulating fluid-rigid body interaction involves solving the Navier-Stokes equations, which describe the flow of fluids. This can be computationally intensive, but techniques such as particle-based methods (e.g., Smoothed Particle Hydrodynamics) and grid-based methods (e.g., Fluid Implicit Particle) are often used to approximate fluid behavior. These methods allow for the simulation of phenomena such as buoyancy, drag, and lift, enhancing the realism of the rigid body simulation.

Advanced rigid body simulation also involves the consideration of material properties and fracture mechanics. Different materials have different physical properties, such as elasticity, plasticity, and brittleness. Accurately modeling these properties requires understanding the material's stress-strain relationship and how it responds to forces. For example, elastic materials return to their original shape after deformation, while plastic materials undergo permanent deformation. Brittle materials, on the other hand, can fracture and break under stress. Simulating fracture mechanics involves determining the conditions under which a material will break and computing the resulting fragments. This adds a layer of complexity to the simulation but is essential for creating realistic destruction effects in games.

Another advanced topic is the simulation of large-scale environments with many interacting rigid bodies. In such scenarios, performance becomes a critical concern. Efficient algorithms and data structures are required to handle the large number of objects and their interactions. Techniques such as parallel computing, level of detail, and adaptive time-stepping are often employed to optimize performance. Parallel computing leverages multiple processors to distribute the computational load, allowing for faster simulations. Level of detail techniques simplify the representation of distant objects, reducing the computational cost without significantly affecting visual quality. Adaptive time-stepping adjusts the simulation time step based on the activity in the scene, using larger time steps for calm periods and smaller time steps for periods of intense interaction.

Lastly, advanced rigid body simulation often involves the integration of machine learning techniques. Machine learning algorithms can be used to predict the behavior of rigid bodies, optimize simulation parameters, and even generate realistic animations. For example, reinforcement learning can be used to train agents to interact with the environment in a physically plausible manner. Neural networks can be used to approximate complex physical models, reducing the computational cost of the simulation. The integration of machine learning techniques opens up new possibilities for creating more intelligent and responsive virtual worlds.

To sum up, advanced topics in rigid body simulation encompass a wide range of techniques and considerations that enhance the realism and complexity of virtual environments. From articulated structures and deformable bodies to collision detection and response, each topic adds a layer of sophistication to the simulation. By incorporating external forces, fluid interactions, material properties, and machine learning, developers can create more dynamic and believable game worlds. The exploration of these advanced topics not only deepens our understanding of rigid body dynamics but also pushes the boundaries of what is possible in game development. Through meticulous implementation and continuous innovation, we can achieve simulations that captivate players and bring virtual worlds to life.

Soft Body Physics: Realistic Deformation And Flexibility

Introduction to Soft Body Physics

Soft body physics is a fascinating and intricate area of game engine theory that focuses on the simulation of materials and objects that exhibit deformable characteristics. Unlike rigid body physics, where objects maintain their shape and structure regardless of external forces, soft body physics deals with objects that can bend, stretch, compress, and twist, providing a more realistic and immersive experience in virtual environments. This capability is crucial for simulating a wide range of phenomena, from the wobble of gelatinous characters to the elasticity of rubber materials and the subtle deformations of human skin.

At its core, soft body physics involves the mathematical modeling of forces and constraints that govern the behavior of flexible materials. These models must account for various physical properties, such as elasticity, plasticity, and damping, to accurately replicate real-world behavior. The complexity of these simulations requires a deep understanding of both physics and computational algorithms, making soft body physics one of the more challenging yet rewarding aspects of game development.

To begin with, it's important to understand the fundamental principles that underpin soft body physics. One of the key concepts is the representation of soft bodies as a network of interconnected nodes or particles. These nodes are often linked by springs or other types of constraints that define how they interact with each other. When an external force is applied to the soft body, such as a collision or a gravitational pull, the nodes respond by moving in a way that respects the constraints, resulting in a deformation of the overall shape.

This particle-based approach allows for a high degree of flexibility and adaptability in simulating various types of soft bodies. For instance, a jelly-like substance can be modeled using a dense network of nodes and springs, resulting in a highly deformable and dynamic object. On the other hand, a more rigid soft body, like a rubber tire, might use stiffer springs and fewer nodes to achieve the desired level of flexibility.

Another important aspect of soft body physics is the handling of collisions and interactions with other objects in the game world. When a soft body comes into contact with a rigid surface or another soft body, the simulation must accurately calculate the resulting forces and deformations. This often involves complex algorithms that take into account the material properties of the interacting objects, such as their mass, friction, and elasticity. Efficiently handling these interactions is crucial for maintaining the realism and performance of the simulation.

One of the main challenges in soft body physics is achieving a balance between realism and computational efficiency. High-fidelity simulations can be extremely resource-intensive, requiring significant processing power and memory. As a result, game developers often need to make trade-offs between the level of detail in the simulation and the performance of the game. Various optimization techniques, such as level-of-detail (LOD) algorithms and parallel processing, can be employed to address these challenges and ensure that the game runs smoothly on a wide range of hardware.

In addition to the technical aspects, soft body physics also plays a crucial role in enhancing the visual and tactile experience of a game. The realistic deformation and flexibility of soft bodies can make characters and objects feel more lifelike and responsive, adding to the overall immersion of the player. For example, the subtle movement of a character's clothing or the squishiness of a soft object can convey important visual cues and contribute to the narrative and emotional impact of the game.

Moreover, soft body physics can be used to create innovative gameplay mechanics and interactions. Games that involve puzzle-solving, exploration, or combat can benefit from the added layer of complexity and realism provided by soft body simulations. For instance, a game might feature a character with stretchy limbs that can be used to solve puzzles or navigate obstacles, or a combat system where the deformation of armor and weapons affects their effectiveness and durability.

In conclusion, soft body physics is a vital component of modern game engine theory, offering a rich and challenging area of study and application. By understanding and leveraging the principles of soft body physics, game developers can create more realistic, immersive, and engaging experiences for players. The ability to simulate deformable materials and objects opens up new possibilities for creativity and innovation in game design, making it an essential tool for any game engine expert. As we continue to push the boundaries of what is possible in virtual environments, the importance of soft body physics will only grow, driving further advancements in both technology and artistry.

Mathematical Models for Soft Body Simulation

Developing mathematical models for simulating deformable objects in virtual environments requires a profound understanding of both physical principles and computational techniques. These models are the foundation of creating convincing and interactive simulations that respond authentically to forces and constraints. This section delves into the various mathematical frameworks and methodologies employed to achieve realistic soft body behavior in game engines.

One of the primary approaches to simulating soft bodies involves the use of continuum mechanics, which describes materials as continuous, rather than discrete, entities. This perspective allows for the modeling of stress, strain, and deformation in a comprehensive manner. The equations governing continuum mechanics, such as the Navier-Stokes equations for fluid dynamics and the Cauchy momentum equation for solid mechanics, provide a robust foundation for simulating a wide range of deformable materials.

Finite Element Analysis (FEA) is a powerful numerical method derived from continuum mechanics. It subdivides a soft body into a mesh of smaller elements, each governed by the same physical laws, but with localized properties that can vary. This discretization allows for the efficient computation of complex deformations and interactions. By solving the equations of motion for each element, FEA can simulate how a soft body responds to various forces, such as gravity, collisions, and user interactions. The accuracy of FEA depends on the resolution of the mesh and the precision of the numerical methods used to solve the equations.

Another widely used technique is the Mass-Spring Model, which represents a soft body as a network of masses connected by springs. Each mass represents a point in the material, and the springs dictate how these points interact with each other. This model simplifies the computation of deformations by reducing the problem to a system of ordinary differential equations, which can be solved using numerical integration methods. The Mass-Spring Model is particularly advantageous for real-time applications, as it strikes a balance between computational efficiency and physical accuracy. Adjusting the stiffness and damping properties of the springs allows developers to fine-tune the behavior of the simulated material to match the desired characteristics.

In addition to the Mass-Spring Model, Position-Based Dynamics (PBD) has gained popularity in recent years for its ability to produce stable and visually plausible simulations. PBD operates by iteratively adjusting the positions of particles to satisfy a set of constraints, rather than directly solving the equations of motion. This approach ensures that the simulated soft body remains stable and free from numerical artifacts, even under complex interactions and high deformation scenarios. PBD is particularly well-suited for interactive applications, such as video games and virtual reality, where real-time performance is crucial.

One of the key challenges in modeling soft bodies is capturing the material's response to external forces in a realistic manner. This involves defining appropriate constitutive models, which describe how the material's stress and strain are related. Common constitutive models include Hookean materials, which exhibit linear elastic behavior, and Neo-Hookean materials, which can model nonlinear elasticity. More advanced models, such as the Mooney-Rivlin and Ogden models, are used to simulate hyperelastic materials, which can undergo large deformations without permanent damage. Selecting the appropriate constitutive model is essential for achieving realistic simulations, as different materials exhibit distinct behaviors under stress.

Incorporating plasticity into soft body simulations adds another layer of complexity. Plasticity refers to the permanent deformation of a material when subjected to forces beyond its elastic limit. Modeling plasticity requires tracking the material's history of deformation and updating its properties accordingly. This is often achieved using techniques such as the Prandtl-Reuss equations, which describe the incremental plastic strain in response to applied stress. Accurately simulating plasticity is crucial for applications where materials undergo permanent changes, such as metal bending or clay sculpting.

Viscoelasticity is another important aspect of soft body simulation, as it combines both elastic and viscous behavior. Viscoelastic materials exhibit time-dependent responses to applied forces, meaning they can slowly deform under a constant load and gradually return to their original shape when the load is removed. This behavior is modeled using constitutive equations that incorporate both elastic and viscous components, such as the Kelvin-Voigt and Maxwell models. Viscoelastic simulations are particularly relevant for materials like biological tissues and polymers, which exhibit both immediate elastic response and gradual flow.

Collision detection and response are critical components of soft body simulation, as interactions with other objects significantly influence the behavior of deformable materials. Efficient collision handling involves detecting intersections between the soft body and other objects, calculating the resulting forces, and updating the simulation accordingly. Techniques such as spatial partitioning and bounding volume hierarchies are used to accelerate collision detection, while penalty-based methods and constraint-based approaches are employed to resolve collisions and ensure realistic interactions.

Optimizing the performance of soft body simulations is essential for achieving real-time interactivity in game engines. This often involves employing parallel processing techniques, such as using GPU acceleration, to distribute the computational workload across multiple processors. Additionally, level-of-detail (LOD) algorithms can be used to dynamically adjust the resolution of the simulation based on the viewer's distance and the importance of the soft body inside the scene. These optimizations help maintain a balance between visual fidelity and computational efficiency, ensuring that the simulation runs smoothly on a wide range of hardware configurations.

To finalize, the mathematical models used for soft body simulation are diverse and multifaceted, each offering unique advantages and trade-offs. From continuum mechanics and finite element analysis to mass-spring models and position-based dynamics, these techniques provide the tools necessary to create realistic and interactive simulations of deformable materials. By carefully selecting and combining these models, game developers can achieve a high degree of realism and responsiveness in their virtual environments, enhancing the overall experience for players. As the field of soft body simulation continues to evolve, new methodologies and optimizations will undoubtedly emerge, further pushing the boundaries of what is possible in game engine theory.

Finite Element Methods in Game Development

Finite Element Methods (FEM) have become a cornerstone in game development, especially when it comes to simulating materials and objects that must exhibit realistic deformation and flexibility. This powerful numerical technique, originally rooted in engineering disciplines such as structural analysis and thermodynamics, has found extensive applications in game engines to bring virtual worlds to life with unprecedented detail and authenticity.

To begin with, it is essential to grasp the fundamental concept behind FEM. At its core, FEM involves breaking down a complex, continuous domain into smaller, simpler parts called elements. These elements are interconnected at points known as nodes. By solving the governing equations of physics at each node and element, FEM enables the simulation of how materials respond to various forces, constraints, and interactions. This modular approach allows for intricate and precise modeling of deformations, making FEM a valuable tool for game developers seeking to create lifelike simulations.

The process of implementing FEM in a game engine starts with the creation of a mesh, which is a discrete representation of the object to be simulated. This mesh is composed of numerous elements, typically in the form of triangles or tetrahedra, depending on whether the object is two-dimensional or three-dimensional. Each element is assigned material properties such as elasticity, density, and damping, which dictate how it behaves under different conditions. The finer the mesh, the more accurately the simulation can capture subtle deformations and interactions. However, this also increases the computational cost, necessitating a balance between detail and performance.

Once the mesh is established, the next step involves defining the governing equations. These equations, derived from principles of continuum mechanics, describe the relationship between forces, displacements, and stresses inside the material. The most common equations used in FEM are the equilibrium equations, which ensure that the sum of forces and moments acting on each element is zero. Additionally, constitutive equations define how the material deforms in response to applied forces, while compatibility equations ensure that the deformation is consistent across the mesh.

Solving these equations for each element and node in the mesh is a computationally intensive task. Game developers often employ numerical methods such as the Galerkin method or the Ritz method to approximate the solutions. These methods involve converting the partial differential equations into a system of algebraic equations that can be solved using techniques like matrix inversion or iterative solvers. The accuracy and stability of the simulation depend on the choice of numerical method and the precision of the computations.

One of the significant advantages of FEM is its versatility in handling a wide range of materials and interactions. For instance, it can simulate the bending and twisting of flexible objects like cloth and paper, the compression and expansion of soft tissues, and the complex deformations of organic materials. This versatility makes FEM particularly well-suited for character animation, where realistic movement and deformation of skin, muscles, and clothing are crucial for creating believable and immersive experiences.

In addition to character animation, FEM plays a vital role in simulating environmental interactions. For example, it can model the deformation of terrain under the weight of a vehicle, the bending of trees in response to wind, and the impact of projectiles on various surfaces. These simulations enhance the realism and dynamism of virtual environments, providing players with a more engaging and interactive experience.

Despite its numerous advantages, the application of FEM in game development is not without challenges. One of the primary challenges is the computational cost associated with solving large systems of equations in real-time. High-fidelity simulations require significant processing power and memory, which can strain the hardware resources of gaming consoles and personal computers. To address this challenge, game developers often employ optimization techniques such as multi-threading, parallel processing, and GPU acceleration. These techniques distribute the computational workload across multiple processors, allowing for faster and more efficient simulations.

Another challenge is the integration of FEM with other simulation techniques commonly used in game engines. For instance, combining FEM with rigid body dynamics, fluid dynamics, and particle systems requires careful coordination to ensure consistent and stable interactions. This often involves developing custom algorithms and data structures that can handle the diverse requirements of different simulation techniques. Achieving seamless integration is crucial for maintaining the overall coherence and performance of the game.

The use of FEM in game development also necessitates a deep understanding of material science and physics. Game developers must carefully select and calibrate material properties to achieve the desired behavior and appearance of simulated objects. This often involves conducting extensive testing and experimentation to fine-tune the parameters and validate the results against real-world observations. Additionally, developers must stay abreast of advancements in FEM research and technology to incorporate the latest techniques and optimizations into their simulations.

In recent years, the advent of machine learning and artificial intelligence has opened new avenues for enhancing FEM simulations. For example, neural networks can be trained to predict the deformation behavior of materials based on historical data, enabling faster and more accurate simulations. Similarly, reinforcement learning algorithms can optimize the placement and properties of mesh elements to achieve specific deformation patterns. These advancements hold the potential to revolutionize the application of FEM in game development, making it more efficient and accessible than ever before.

In conclusion, Finite Element Methods are a powerful and versatile tool for simulating realistic deformation and flexibility in game development. By breaking down complex objects into smaller elements and solving the governing equations of physics, FEM enables the creation of lifelike and interactive simulations that enhance the immersion and engagement of virtual worlds. Despite the challenges associated with computational cost and integration, the continued advancement of FEM technology and techniques promises to unlock new possibilities for creativity and innovation in game design. As game developers continue to push the boundaries of what is possible, FEM will undoubtedly remain a cornerstone of realistic and dynamic simulations in the ever-evolving landscape of game engine theory.

In the realm of interactive digital environments, the capacity to manage collisions involving soft bodies in real-time is a critical aspect that significantly enhances the realism and immersion of a game. This section delves into the intricacies of handling collisions for deformable objects, focusing on the methods and techniques that enable accurate and efficient simulations.

The initial step in real-time soft body collision handling involves the detection of potential intersections between soft bodies and other entities inside the game world. This process, known as collision detection, is inherently more complex for soft bodies than for rigid bodies due to their deformable nature. Unlike rigid bodies that maintain a constant shape, soft bodies can change form dynamically, necessitating a more sophisticated approach to accurately identify collisions.

One effective method for collision detection in soft bodies is the use of bounding volumes. Bounding volumes are simplified geometric shapes that encapsulate the more complex soft body, providing a preliminary check for potential collisions. Common types of bounding volumes include axis-aligned bounding boxes (AABBs), oriented bounding boxes (OBBs), and spheres. These volumes are computationally inexpensive to test for intersections, making them suitable for the initial phase of collision detection.

Once a potential collision is identified using bounding volumes, a more detailed examination is required to determine the exact points of contact and the extent of the intersection. This is typically achieved through techniques such as mesh-based collision detection, where the surface of the soft body is represented by a mesh of interconnected vertices. By analyzing the interactions between the vertices of the soft body and the surfaces of other objects, precise collision points can be identified.

With the collision points determined, the next step is to calculate the response of the soft body to the collision. This involves determining the forces and deformations that result from the interaction. One approach to handling collision response is the penalty method, where a virtual force is applied to the colliding points to push them apart. The magnitude of this force is proportional to the degree of penetration, ensuring that the soft body responds in a manner that reflects the severity of the collision.

An alternative to the penalty method is the constraint-based approach, which enforces positional constraints on the colliding points to prevent them from penetrating each other. This method involves solving a system of equations that describe the constraints, ensuring that the positions of the colliding points are adjusted to satisfy the non-penetration condition. Constraint-based methods are often more stable and produce more visually plausible results, particularly for complex interactions and high-deformation scenarios.

In addition to handling the immediate response to collisions, it is also important to consider the long-term effects of repeated interactions. Soft bodies may exhibit behaviors such as stress accumulation, fatigue, and permanent deformation, which need to be accounted for in the simulation. Incorporating these effects requires a detailed understanding of the material properties of the soft body and the development of models that can accurately predict how the material will respond over time.

One technique for modeling long-term effects is the use of viscoelastic materials, which combine both elastic and viscous properties. Viscoelastic materials can gradually deform under a constant load and slowly return to their original shape when the load is removed. By incorporating viscoelastic models into the collision handling process, it is possible to simulate realistic behaviors such as gradual sagging, creeping, and recovery, which add to the overall realism of the simulation.

Another important aspect of real-time soft body collision handling is the optimization of the computational process to ensure that the simulation can run efficiently on a wide range of hardware. Techniques such as spatial partitioning, where the game world is divided into smaller regions, can significantly reduce the number of collision checks required by limiting the scope of the detection process to relevant areas. Additionally, leveraging parallel processing capabilities of modern GPUs can distribute the computational load, enabling faster and more efficient simulations.

Moreover, adaptive algorithms that dynamically adjust the level of detail in the simulation based on the viewer's perspective and the importance of the soft body in the scene can further enhance performance. By reducing the complexity of distant or less significant objects, these algorithms ensure that computational resources are prioritized for the most critical elements, maintaining a balance between visual fidelity and efficiency.

In summary, real-time soft body collision handling is a multifaceted challenge that requires a combination of sophisticated detection, response, and optimization techniques. By effectively managing collisions, game developers can create more immersive and realistic virtual environments, enhancing the player's experience. The continuous advancement of computational methods and hardware capabilities promises to further refine these techniques, pushing the boundaries of what is possible in real-time soft body simulations.

Material Properties and Deformation

In game engine theory, the accurate simulation of soft body physics hinges significantly on the comprehensive understanding of material properties and their impact on deformation. This section delves into the critical aspects of how various material characteristics influence the behavior of deformable objects inside virtual environments, aiming to provide a detailed exploration that spans multiple dimensions of this intricate subject.

To begin with, the intrinsic properties of materials dictate how they respond to external forces, which in turn affects their deformation. These properties include elasticity, plasticity, and viscosity, each playing a crucial role in defining the material's overall behavior. Elasticity refers to a material's ability to return to its original shape after the removal of an applied force. This property is often quantified using parameters such as Young's modulus, which measures the stiffness of the material, and Poisson's ratio, which describes the ratio of transverse strain to axial strain. Materials with high elasticity, such as rubber, can undergo significant deformations and still revert to their initial form, making them ideal for simulating objects like bouncing balls or flexible joints.

On the other hand, plasticity pertains to the permanent deformation that occurs when a material is subjected to forces beyond its elastic limit. This property is particularly relevant for materials that experience irreversible changes in shape, such as clay or metal under high stress. The yield strength of a material, which indicates the stress level at which plastic deformation begins, is a key parameter in modeling plastic behavior. Understanding and accurately simulating plasticity is essential for creating realistic interactions in scenarios where materials are permanently altered, such as in crash simulations or sculpting applications.

Viscosity, the measure of a material's resistance to flow, adds another layer of complexity to soft body simulations. Viscous materials, like honey or tar, exhibit time-dependent deformation, meaning they gradually change shape under a constant load and slowly return to their original form once the load is removed. The viscosity coefficient is a critical parameter in capturing this behavior, influencing how quickly or slowly the material deforms. Incorporating viscosity into soft body simulations allows for the realistic portrayal of materials that exhibit both immediate elastic response and gradual flow, such as biological tissues or polymers.

Beyond these fundamental properties, the behavior of materials under deformation is also influenced by their internal structure and composition. For instance, composite materials, which consist of two or more distinct substances combined to achieve specific properties, can exhibit unique deformation characteristics. The interaction between the different components of the composite, such as the matrix and the reinforcement, plays a crucial role in determining the material's overall response to applied forces. Simulating the behavior of composite materials requires a detailed understanding of their microstructure and the interactions between their constituents.

In addition to the intrinsic properties and internal structure, external factors such as temperature and strain rate can significantly impact material deformation. Temperature variations can alter the mechanical properties of materials, affecting their elasticity, plasticity, and viscosity. For example, metals typically become more ductile at higher temperatures, allowing for greater deformation before failure. Similarly, the rate at which a material is deformed, known as the strain rate, can influence its response. Materials subjected to rapid deformation often exhibit different behaviors compared to those deformed slowly, necessitating the incorporation of strain rate effects into the simulation models.

The accurate representation of material properties in soft body simulations requires the development and implementation of sophisticated mathematical models. These models, often derived from principles of continuum mechanics, describe the relationship between forces, displacements, and stresses inside the material. Constitutive equations, which define how the material deforms in response to applied forces, are a critical component of these models. Various types of constitutive equations exist, ranging from simple linear models to complex nonlinear formulations, each suited to different types of materials and deformation scenarios.

One common approach to modeling material deformation is the use of hyperelastic models, which are particularly well-suited for materials that undergo large deformations without permanent damage. Hyperelastic models, such as the Mooney-Rivlin and Ogden models, describe the material's stress-strain relationship using strain energy density functions. These functions capture the nonlinear elastic behavior of the material, allowing for accurate simulation of large deformations. Hyperelastic models are often used in applications involving rubber-like materials, where capturing the material's ability to stretch significantly and return to its original shape is crucial.

Another approach involves the use of viscoelastic models, which combine both elastic and viscous components to describe the material's time-dependent behavior. Viscoelastic models, such as the Kelvin-Voigt and Maxwell models, incorporate parameters that account for both the immediate elastic response and the gradual flow of the material. These models are particularly useful for simulating materials like biological tissues, which exhibit both elasticity and viscosity. By accurately capturing the time-dependent deformation behavior, viscoelastic models enhance the realism of soft body simulations in applications such as medical simulations or character animations.

Incorporating plasticity into material models adds another layer of complexity, as it requires tracking the material's history of deformation and updating its properties accordingly. Incremental plasticity models, such as the Prandtl-Reuss equations, describe the incremental plastic strain in response to applied stress. These models often involve the use of yield criteria, which define the conditions under which plastic deformation begins, and hardening rules, which describe how the material's resistance to deformation evolves with continued loading. Accurate simulation of plasticity is essential for applications involving permanent changes in shape, such as metal forming or damage modeling.

The implementation of these mathematical models in game engines involves discretizing the continuous material domain into smaller, manageable elements. This discretization process, often achieved using techniques such as finite element methods or particle-based methods, allows for the efficient computation of deformations and interactions. Each element or particle is assigned material properties and governed by the constitutive equations, enabling the simulation of how the material responds to various forces and constraints. The resolution of the discretization, or the level of detail in the mesh or particle system, significantly impacts the accuracy and performance of the simulation.

In addition to the mathematical models, the accurate simulation of material deformation also relies on robust numerical methods for solving the governing equations. Techniques such as finite difference methods, finite volume methods, and spectral methods are commonly used to approximate the solutions of the partial differential equations that describe the material behavior. The choice of numerical method and the precision of the computations play a crucial role in determining the stability and accuracy of the simulation. Efficient numerical solvers, such as iterative methods or direct solvers, are often employed to handle the large systems of equations that arise in soft body simulations.

Optimizing the performance of soft body simulations requires a careful balance between accuracy and computational efficiency. Techniques such as adaptive mesh refinement, where the resolution of the mesh is dynamically adjusted based on the deformation characteristics, can enhance the accuracy of the simulation while maintaining computational efficiency. Additionally, leveraging the parallel processing capabilities of modern hardware, such as GPUs, can significantly accelerate the computation, enabling real-time simulations of complex deformable objects.

To summarize, the accurate simulation of material properties and deformation is a multifaceted challenge that requires a deep understanding of the intrinsic properties, internal structure, and external factors that influence material behavior. By developing and implementing sophisticated mathematical models and numerical methods, game developers can create realistic and interactive simulations of deformable objects, enhancing the overall immersion and engagement of virtual environments. As the field of soft body physics continues to evolve, ongoing advancements in material modeling and computational techniques promise to unlock new possibilities for creativity and innovation in game engine theory.

Optimizing Soft Body Performance for Real-Time Applications

In the dynamic landscape of interactive digital environments, achieving realistic deformation and flexibility for soft bodies while maintaining real-time performance is a critical challenge. This section delves into the various strategies and techniques employed to optimize the performance of soft body simulations, ensuring they run efficiently on contemporary hardware without compromising on realism.

One of the primary considerations in optimizing soft body performance is the choice of the underlying computational framework. Different simulation frameworks offer varying trade-offs between accuracy and computational efficiency. For instance, mass-spring models, which represent soft bodies as networks of masses connected by springs, can provide a good balance between simplicity and performance. These models are relatively straightforward to implement and can be computed efficiently, making them suitable for real-time applications. However, they may lack the detailed accuracy required for complex deformations, necessitating the use of more advanced methods in certain scenarios.

Another crucial aspect of optimization is the efficient handling of collision detection. Soft bodies, due to their deformable nature, require more sophisticated collision detection algorithms compared to rigid bodies. One effective approach is the use of hierarchical spatial partitioning techniques, such as bounding volume hierarchies (BVH) or spatial grids. These methods divide the game world into smaller regions, allowing for rapid identification of potential collision pairs. By narrowing down the number of collision checks to only those that are relevant, these techniques significantly reduce the computational load, enhancing overall performance.

In addition to spatial partitioning, level of detail (LOD) techniques play a vital role in optimizing soft body simulations. LOD methods dynamically adjust the complexity of the simulation based on the viewer's perspective and the importance of the soft body inside the scene. For instance, objects that are far away or less critical to the gameplay can be represented with lower resolution meshes, while those in close proximity or of higher significance are simulated with greater detail. This adaptive approach ensures that computational resources are allocated efficiently, prioritizing the most visually impactful elements without overwhelming the hardware.

Parallel processing is another powerful tool for optimizing soft body performance. Modern graphics processing units (GPUs) are capable of executing many operations simultaneously, making them well-suited for the parallel nature of soft body simulations. By distributing the computational workload across multiple processing units, GPUs can handle complex simulations more efficiently than traditional central processing units (CPUs). Techniques such as CUDA (Compute Unified Device Architecture) and OpenCL (Open Computing Language) enable developers to leverage the parallel processing capabilities of GPUs, significantly accelerating the simulation process.

Furthermore, multi-threading can be employed to take advantage of multi-core CPUs. By dividing the simulation tasks into smaller, independent threads that can run concurrently, multi-threading allows for better utilization of the available processing power. This approach is particularly beneficial for tasks that can be parallelized, such as collision detection and force computations. Properly managing thread synchronization and minimizing data dependencies are crucial to ensure smooth and efficient execution of multi-threaded simulations.

Memory management is another critical factor in optimizing soft body performance. Efficient use of memory can significantly impact the speed and responsiveness of the simulation. Techniques such as memory pooling, where a fixed block of memory is allocated and reused for different simulation elements, can reduce the overhead associated with frequent memory allocation and deallocation. Additionally, minimizing cache misses by organizing data structures to take advantage of spatial locality can enhance memory access patterns, further improving performance.

Another optimization strategy involves the use of approximation techniques to simplify complex calculations. For instance, precomputed deformation patterns or lookup tables can be used to approximate the behavior of soft bodies under certain conditions, reducing the need for real-time computation. While these approximations may sacrifice some degree of accuracy, they can provide substantial performance gains, making them a viable option for scenarios where real-time responsiveness is paramount.

In real-time applications, it is also essential to implement robust error handling and stability measures. Numerical instability can lead to unrealistic deformations or even simulation crashes, undermining the overall experience. Techniques such as implicit integration methods, which provide greater numerical stability compared to explicit methods, can help mitigate these issues. Additionally, applying constraints and regularization techniques to enforce physical plausibility can prevent excessive deformation and maintain the integrity of the simulation.

Profiling and performance analysis tools are invaluable for identifying bottlenecks and optimizing soft body simulations. By systematically analyzing the performance of different components of the simulation, developers can pinpoint areas that require optimization and implement targeted improvements. Tools such as NVIDIA Nsight, Intel VTune, and AMD CodeXL offer detailed insights into GPU and CPU performance, enabling developers to fine-tune their simulations for maximum efficiency.

Lastly, continuous testing and iterative refinement are essential for achieving optimal performance in soft body simulations. The complexity of real-time applications necessitates a rigorous testing process to ensure that optimizations do not introduce unintended side effects or degrade the quality of the simulation. By iteratively refining the simulation based on performance metrics and user feedback, developers can strike a balance between realism and efficiency, delivering a seamless and immersive experience.

Essentially, optimizing soft body performance for real-time applications involves a multifaceted approach that encompasses computational frameworks, collision detection, level of detail techniques, parallel processing, memory management, approximation methods, stability measures, and performance analysis. By leveraging these strategies, developers can create realistic and responsive soft body simulations that enhance the overall immersion and interactivity of digital environments. As hardware capabilities continue to evolve, ongoing advancements in optimization techniques promise to further push the boundaries of what is possible in real-time soft body physics.

Case Studies: Implementing Soft Body Physics in Popular Games

Exploring the practical application of soft body physics in well-known games provides invaluable insights into the challenges and successes of integrating realistic deformation and flexibility. This section examines several case studies, highlighting the innovative techniques and solutions employed by developers to bring lifelike soft body dynamics to their virtual worlds.

Case Study 1: "Red Dead Redemption 2" - The Realism of Natural Environments
"Red Dead Redemption 2," developed by Rockstar Games, is celebrated for its breathtaking realism and attention to detail. One of the standout features is its sophisticated physics engine, which includes impressive soft body dynamics. The game's natural environments, such as the behavior of animal bodies and the interaction of characters with various terrain types, showcase advanced soft body simulations.

In "Red Dead Redemption 2," the developers utilized a combination of procedural animation and physics-based modeling to achieve lifelike movements and deformations. For instance, when a player hunts and harvests animals, the carcasses exhibit realistic sagging and deformation, adhering to the principles of soft body physics. This approach required the integration of skeletal animations with a flexible mesh that could respond to external forces, providing a seamless blend of pre-defined motions and real-time physical reactions.

The game also features dynamic weather conditions and terrain interactions that affect the behavior of soft bodies. Characters and animals leave imprints in snow, mud, and water, with the surfaces deforming realistically under their weight. Achieving this level of detail involved extensive use of texture blending and displacement mapping, allowing the environment to adapt dynamically to the presence of soft bodies.

Case Study 2: "The Last of Us Part II" - Enhancing Emotional Impact with Soft Body Physics

Naughty Dog's "The Last of Us Part II" is renowned for its emotional storytelling and immersive gameplay. A critical component of this immersion is the game's use of soft body physics to enhance character interactions and environmental realism. The developers aimed to create a world where every element, from clothing to facial expressions, responded naturally to physical forces.

One significant application of soft body physics in "The Last of Us Part II" is in the simulation of character clothing and gear. The game's characters wear multiple layers of clothing that move and deform independently, reacting to the characters' movements and external forces such as wind and water. This was achieved through a combination of cloth simulation techniques and collision detection algorithms, ensuring that the fabric behaved realistically without clipping through other objects.

Another notable implementation is the use of soft body physics in facial animations. The developers employed a blend of muscle simulation and morph target animation to create highly expressive faces that could convey a wide range of emotions. This approach allowed for subtle deformations in the skin and underlying muscle structures, providing a more believable and emotionally engaging experience.

Case Study 3: "BeamNG.drive" - Pushing the Limits of Vehicle Physics

"BeamNG.drive," developed by BeamNG GmbH, is a driving simulation game that stands out for its highly detailed and realistic vehicle physics. Unlike traditional racing games, "BeamNG.drive" focuses on the accurate simulation of vehicle dynamics, including soft body physics for car deformations during collisions and impacts.

The core of "BeamNG.drive's" soft body physics is its node-beam structure, which represents vehicles as networks of interconnected nodes and beams. This structure allows for realistic deformation and flexibility, enabling vehicles to bend, crumple, and break apart in response to collisions. The developers designed a comprehensive physics model that accounts for various material properties, such as metal fatigue and plastic deformation, resulting in highly detailed and varied damage outcomes.

To achieve real-time performance, the game employs optimization techniques such as adaptive time-stepping and parallel processing. These methods ensure that the complex calculations required for soft body physics do not overwhelm the system, allowing for smooth and responsive gameplay even during intense crash scenarios.

Case Study 4: "Spider-Man" - Realistic Web-Swinging and Character Dynamics
Insomniac Games' "Spider-Man" showcases another innovative use of soft body physics, particularly in the context of web-swinging and character dynamics. The game's portrayal of Spider-Man's acrobatic movements and interactions with the environment relies heavily on advanced physics simulations.

One of the key challenges in "Spider-Man" was creating a believable web-swinging mechanic that adhered to the laws of physics while still providing a fun and fluid gameplay experience. The developers implemented a blend of procedural animation and physics-based constraints to simulate the tension and flexibility of Spider-Man's webs. This approach allowed the webs to stretch and bend realistically, reacting to Spider-Man's velocity and the surrounding environment.

Additionally, the game's character dynamics benefited from soft body physics, particularly in the simulation of Spider-Man's costume and musculature. The developers used a combination of cloth simulation and muscle deformation to achieve natural-looking movements and interactions. This allowed the character's body to respond dynamically to various forces, enhancing the overall realism and immersion.

Case Study 5: "Inside" - Atmospheric Puzzles and Soft Body Interactions

"Inside," developed by Playdead, is an atmospheric puzzle-platformer that employs soft body physics to create unique and engaging gameplay mechanics. The game's dark and moody aesthetic is complemented by its innovative use of physics-based interactions, particularly in the context of the protagonist's movements and environmental puzzles.

In "Inside," soft body physics are used to simulate the protagonist's interactions with various objects and obstacles. For example, the character's body deforms realistically when squeezing through tight spaces or pushing against heavy objects. This was achieved through a combination of skeletal animation and real-time physics simulation, allowing for fluid and natural-looking movements.

The game also features puzzles that rely on the realistic behavior of soft bodies. One notable example is a sequence where the protagonist must navigate through a series of water-filled chambers. The water's surface deforms and reacts to the character's movements, creating a dynamic and immersive puzzle-solving experience. This required the integration of fluid dynamics with soft body physics, providing a cohesive and believable interaction between the character and the environment.

Conclusion

These case studies illustrate the diverse and innovative ways in which soft body physics can be implemented in popular games to enhance realism and immersion. From the natural environments of "Red Dead Redemption 2" to the vehicle dynamics of "BeamNG.drive," the use of soft body physics allows developers to create more lifelike and engaging experiences. By examining these examples, we gain valuable insights into the techniques and challenges involved in bringing realistic deformation and flexibility to interactive digital worlds.

Collision Detection And Response: Ensuring Realistic Interactions

Fundamentals of Collision Detection Algorithms

In interactive digital experiences, collision detection algorithms form the backbone of realistic gameplay. These algorithms ensure that virtual objects behave in ways that mimic the physical world, contributing to the immersion and believability of the game environment. This section delves into the core principles and methodologies that underpin collision detection algorithms, providing a comprehensive understanding necessary for creating precise and efficient simulations.

At its essence, collision detection is the computational problem of detecting when two or more objects intersect or come into contact inside a virtual space. This task, while seemingly straightforward, involves a variety of complex challenges, especially as the number of objects and the intricacy of their shapes increase. To manage these challenges, several fundamental techniques and strategies have been developed over the years.

One of the most basic and widely used methods is the Axis-Aligned Bounding Box (AABB) algorithm. This technique simplifies objects into rectangular boxes aligned with the coordinate axes, making it easy to determine overlaps through simple comparisons of their min and max extents along each axis. While AABBs are computationally inexpensive, they are most effective for objects that can be reasonably approximated by boxes and can become less accurate with irregularly shaped or rotating objects.

To address the limitations of AABBs, the Oriented Bounding Box (OBB) algorithm was introduced. Unlike AABBs, OBBs are not constrained to align with the coordinate axes, allowing them to better fit the contours of the objects they encapsulate. This flexibility comes at the cost of increased computational complexity, as determining overlaps between OBBs involves more intricate mathematical operations, including the Separating Axis Theorem (SAT). SAT is a crucial concept in collision detection, providing a robust method to test if two convex shapes intersect by projecting them onto potential separating axes.

For more detailed and precise collision detection, especially in complex environments, the use of spatial partitioning techniques like Binary Space Partitioning (BSP) trees and Quadtrees is common. These methods divide the game world into hierarchical segments, enabling more efficient querying and reducing the number of collision checks needed. BSP trees, for instance, recursively split the space into convex sets by hyperplanes, which can be particularly advantageous in static environments like architectural structures. Quadtrees, on the other hand, divide the space into four quadrants, making them suitable for dynamic scenes with varying levels of detail.

Another pivotal approach in collision detection is the use of bounding volumes hierarchies (BVH). This technique constructs a tree of nested bounding volumes, each encapsulating a group of objects or sub-volumes. By traversing this tree, the algorithm can quickly eliminate large sets of objects from collision checks, focusing only on those inside intersecting volumes. BVHs are especially effective for scenes with a large number of objects, as they significantly reduce the computational load by culling non-colliding pairs early in the process.

In addition to these methods, continuous collision detection (CCD) plays a vital role in ensuring realistic interactions, particularly for fast-moving objects. Unlike discrete collision detection, which checks for collisions at fixed time intervals, CCD considers the entire motion path of objects, preventing the common issue of "tunneling" where fast objects pass through each other between frames. Techniques like swept volumes and time of impact calculations are employed to accurately detect and respond to collisions over continuous motion.

The choice of collision detection algorithm depends on various factors, including the complexity of the game world, the number of interacting objects, and the required level of precision. For instance, simple arcade games with few objects may suffice with basic AABB checks, while high-fidelity simulations or physics-based puzzles might necessitate the use of BVHs or CCD techniques.

Understanding these fundamental algorithms and their appropriate applications is crucial for any game developer aiming to create believable and responsive interactions in their virtual worlds. As we continue to explore the intricacies of collision detection, it becomes evident that this field is a blend of mathematical rigor, computational efficiency, and creative problem-solving, all working together to bring digital environments to life.

In summary, the fundamentals of collision detection algorithms encompass a range of techniques from simple bounding boxes to complex hierarchical structures and continuous detection methods. Each approach offers unique advantages and challenges, and their effective implementation is key to achieving realistic and immersive gameplay. Through a deep dive into these algorithms, developers can gain the insights needed to choose and optimize the best collision detection strategies for their specific game projects.

Broad-Phase vs. Narrow-Phase Collision Detection

In the grand architecture of collision detection inside game engines, a well-structured approach is essential to balance accuracy and computational efficiency. This balance is typically achieved through a two-phase process: the broad-phase and the narrow-phase. Each of these phases plays a distinct and critical role in the detection and resolution of interactions between objects in a virtual environment. Understanding the differences and the interplay between these phases is fundamental for any game developer aiming to create realistic and responsive game worlds.

The broad-phase collision detection serves as the initial filter in the collision detection pipeline. Its primary function is to quickly eliminate pairs of objects that are definitely not colliding, thereby reducing the number of potential collisions that need to be examined in more detail. This phase is crucial for optimizing performance, especially in complex scenes with numerous objects. By efficiently culling non-colliding pairs, the broad-phase significantly minimizes the computational load on the subsequent narrow-phase.

Several techniques are employed in the broad-phase to achieve this initial filtering. One common method is the use of spatial partitioning, which involves dividing the game world into a grid or a hierarchical structure. For instance, a uniform grid partitions the space into cells, and objects are assigned to these cells based on their positions. By only checking for collisions between objects inside the same or neighboring cells, the algorithm reduces the number of potential interactions. This method is particularly effective in scenarios where objects are evenly distributed across the space.

Another widely used technique in the broad-phase is sweep and prune, also known as sort and sweep. This method sorts objects along one or more axes and then checks for overlapping intervals. By leveraging the sorted order, the algorithm can efficiently identify potential collisions without needing to compare every pair of objects. Sweep and prune is especially advantageous in dynamic environments where objects are frequently moving, as it can quickly update the sorted lists and maintain efficient collision checks.

Bounding volume hierarchies (BVHs) also play a significant role in the broad-phase. These hierarchical structures group objects into nested bounding volumes, allowing for rapid elimination of non-colliding pairs. By traversing the hierarchy, the algorithm can focus on more promising regions of the game world, thereby reducing the number of detailed collision checks needed in the narrow-phase. BVHs are particularly useful in scenes with large numbers of objects, as they effectively manage the complexity by culling broad regions of space.

Once the broad-phase has filtered out the majority of non-colliding pairs, the narrow-phase collision detection takes over. This phase is responsible for performing precise and detailed checks on the remaining potential collisions identified by the broad-phase. The narrow-phase employs more computationally intensive algorithms to accurately determine whether the objects are indeed colliding and to calculate the exact points of contact.

In the narrow-phase, various algorithms are used depending on the shapes and properties of the objects involved. For simple geometric shapes, such as spheres or boxes, analytical methods can be used to determine collisions with high precision. These methods involve mathematical formulas that directly calculate the intersection points based on the objects' dimensions and positions.

For more complex shapes, the narrow-phase often relies on polygonal mesh collision detection. This approach involves checking for intersections between the polygons that make up the objects' surfaces. Algorithms such as the Gilbert-Johnson-Keerthi (GJK) algorithm are commonly used for this purpose. The GJK algorithm is particularly effective for convex shapes, as it iteratively searches for the closest points between two objects and determines whether they intersect.

In addition to detecting collisions, the narrow-phase also handles collision response, which involves calculating the appropriate reactions to detected collisions. This may include determining the forces and impulses to be applied to the objects to resolve the collision and ensure realistic interactions. Various techniques are used for this purpose, such as impulse-based methods, which calculate the change in velocity needed to separate the objects, and penalty-based methods, which apply corrective forces to resolve interpenetrations.

The effectiveness of the collision detection pipeline relies on the seamless integration of the broad-phase and narrow-phase. The broad-phase must efficiently filter out non-colliding pairs to minimize the workload on the narrow-phase, while the narrow-phase must accurately and precisely handle the remaining potential collisions. Together, these phases ensure that collision detection is both computationally efficient and capable of producing realistic and believable interactions.

In summary, the distinction between broad-phase and narrow-phase collision detection is a cornerstone of efficient and accurate collision handling in game engines. The broad-phase serves as a preliminary filter to reduce the number of potential collisions, while the narrow-phase conducts detailed and precise checks on the remaining pairs. By understanding and effectively implementing these phases, developers can create game worlds that are both responsive and immersive, providing players with a seamless and realistic experience.

Handling Complex Interactions in Game Physics

In the dynamic world of game development, simulating intricate interactions between objects is a vital aspect of creating believable environments. The complexity of these interactions can vary significantly, from simple bouncing balls to the intricate dynamics of a collapsing building. Addressing these sophisticated scenarios requires a deep understanding of both the physical principles involved and the computational techniques that can efficiently replicate them inside a virtual space.

One of the primary challenges in handling complex interactions is managing the multitude of forces and constraints that can act on objects. For instance, when simulating a stack of blocks, each block is subject to gravitational forces, contact forces from adjacent blocks, and potentially frictional forces that resist sliding. These forces must be calculated accurately to ensure the stack behaves in a realistic manner, whether it topples over or remains stable under external influences.

To achieve this, game physics engines often employ a combination of rigid body dynamics and constraint solvers. Rigid body dynamics is a fundamental concept in physics engines, where objects are treated as solid, non-deformable entities. This simplification allows for more straightforward calculations of motion and interactions. However, to accurately simulate complex interactions, it is crucial to incorporate constraint solvers that enforce specific conditions, such as maintaining the structural integrity of a bridge or ensuring that characters' limbs move naturally.

Constraint solvers come in various forms, with one of the most widely used being the

Jacobian-based method. This approach involves defining constraints in terms of Jacobian matrices, which describe the relationship between the forces applied to an object and the resulting accelerations. By solving these matrices iteratively, the physics engine can ensure that all constraints are satisfied, resulting in realistic and stable interactions. This method is particularly effective for handling articulated structures, such as ragdolls or mechanical systems, where multiple interconnected parts must move cohesively.

Another critical aspect of handling complex interactions is the accurate simulation of contact and friction. When two objects come into contact, the physics engine must determine the exact points of contact and the resulting forces. This process is known as contact resolution and is essential for preventing objects from interpenetrating and for generating realistic responses, such as bouncing or sliding. Advanced contact resolution algorithms, such as the Projected Gauss-Seidel (PGS) method, are often employed to handle multiple contact points simultaneously, ensuring stable and realistic interactions even in densely packed environments.

Friction, on the other hand, is a force that resists the relative motion of two surfaces in contact. It plays a crucial role in many game scenarios, from characters walking on different surfaces to vehicles navigating challenging terrains. Accurate friction modeling requires considering both static friction, which prevents objects from starting to move, and dynamic friction, which resists ongoing motion. These forces are typically modeled using Coulomb's law of friction, which provides a simple yet effective way to calculate the frictional forces based on the normal force and a coefficient of friction.

In addition to rigid body dynamics, soft body dynamics is another area of game physics that deals with deformable objects. Unlike rigid bodies, soft bodies can change shape in response to forces, making them suitable for simulating materials like cloth, jelly, or even human tissue. Soft body dynamics involves solving complex systems of partial differential equations to determine how forces propagate through the material and cause deformations. Techniques such as the Finite Element Method (FEM) or Mass-Spring systems are commonly used to discretize these equations and simulate the behavior of soft bodies in real-time.

Handling complex interactions also requires efficient collision detection algorithms, particularly for objects with intricate shapes or large numbers of interacting components. Hierarchical data structures, such as Bounding Volume Hierarchies (BVH) or k-DOP trees, are often used to accelerate collision detection by organizing objects into nested groups. These structures allow the physics engine to quickly eliminate large sets of non-colliding objects and focus on the detailed interactions between those that are likely to intersect.

Moreover, continuous collision detection (CCD) techniques are essential for accurately simulating fast-moving objects. Unlike traditional methods that check for collisions at discrete time intervals, CCD tracks the entire motion path of objects, ensuring that collisions are detected and resolved even when objects move rapidly. This approach prevents issues such as tunneling, where fast-moving objects pass through each other without being detected, and is crucial for maintaining the realism of high-speed interactions.

The complexity of interactions in game physics also extends to fluid dynamics, where the behavior of liquids and gases must be simulated. Fluid dynamics involves solving the Navier-Stokes equations, which describe how the velocity field of a fluid evolves over time.

These equations are highly complex and require sophisticated numerical methods, such as Smoothed Particle Hydrodynamics (SPH) or grid-based solvers, to approximate their solutions. Fluid simulations are used in various game scenarios, from simulating water flows and splashes to creating realistic smoke and fire effects.

Another important consideration in handling complex interactions is the integration of physics with other game systems, such as animation and AI. For instance, character animations must be driven by the underlying physics engine to ensure that movements are natural and responsive to the environment. This requires a seamless integration of inverse kinematics (IK) systems, which calculate the necessary joint angles to achieve a desired end position, with the physics engine's constraint solvers. Similarly, AI systems must take into account physical interactions when planning and executing actions, such as navigating obstacles or engaging in combat.

Essentially, handling complex interactions in game physics is a multifaceted challenge that requires a deep understanding of physical principles and computational techniques. By employing advanced methods for rigid body dynamics, constraint solving, contact resolution, friction modeling, soft body dynamics, collision detection, fluid dynamics, and system integration, developers can create highly realistic and immersive game environments. These techniques not only enhance the believability of the virtual world but also provide players with engaging and dynamic experiences that respond authentically to their actions.

Efficient Data Structures for Collision Detection

In the intricate world of game development, ensuring that objects interact realistically requires not only sophisticated collision detection algorithms but also the use of efficient data structures. These data structures are critical in managing the spatial relationships between objects, enabling quick and accurate identification of potential collisions. This section explores various data structures that are pivotal in optimizing collision detection processes, thereby enhancing both the performance and realism of interactive digital environments.

Spatial partitioning is a foundational approach in organizing objects inside a game world. This technique divides the space into manageable sections, allowing for more efficient querying and reducing the computational load when checking for potential collisions. One of the simplest forms of spatial partitioning is the uniform grid. In this method, the game world is divided into a grid of equal-sized cells, and objects are assigned to these cells based on their positions. When checking for collisions, the algorithm only needs to consider objects inside the same cell or adjacent cells, significantly reducing the number of comparisons needed. This approach is particularly effective in scenarios where objects are evenly distributed and move predictably.

However, uniform grids can become less efficient in environments with highly variable object densities. To address this, hierarchical spatial partitioning techniques like Quadtrees and Octrees are employed. Quadtrees divide the two-dimensional space into four quadrants recursively, while Octrees extend this concept to three-dimensional spaces by dividing it into eight octants. These hierarchical structures allow for more adaptive partitioning, where regions with higher object densities are subdivided further, enabling more efficient collision checks. By focusing computational resources on densely populated areas, Quadtrees and Octrees provide a balanced approach to managing spatial complexity.

Another powerful data structure in collision detection is the bounding volume hierarchy (BVH). BVHs organize objects into a tree of nested bounding volumes, each encapsulating a group of objects or sub-volumes. The primary advantage of BVHs is their ability to quickly exclude large sets of non-colliding objects by traversing the hierarchy. When checking for collisions, the algorithm starts from the root of the tree and descends through the hierarchy, focusing only on intersecting volumes. This hierarchical approach significantly reduces the number of detailed collision checks needed, making BVHs highly effective for scenes with a large number of objects.

In addition to BVHs, k-DOP trees (Discrete Oriented Polytopes) offer another hierarchical structure for efficient collision detection. k-DOPs generalize bounding volumes by using a fixed number of oriented planes to create a convex polytope that tightly fits the object. These structures can provide a more accurate approximation of an object's shape compared to traditional bounding boxes, leading to fewer false positives in collision checks. k-DOP trees leverage this accuracy by organizing objects into a hierarchical structure similar to BVHs, enabling efficient traversal and collision detection.

For dynamic environments where objects frequently move and interact, dynamic data structures like the sweep and prune algorithm are particularly useful. This method involves sorting objects along one or more axes and then checking for overlapping intervals. As objects move, the sorted order is updated, allowing for efficient identification of potential collisions. Sweep and prune is especially advantageous in scenarios with frequent object movements, as it maintains an up-to-date list of potential collisions with minimal computational overhead.

Another dynamic data structure is the spatial hash, which maps objects to a hash table based on their positions. Spatial hashing allows for quick insertion, deletion, and querying of objects, making it suitable for real-time applications. When checking for collisions, the algorithm only needs to consider objects inside the same hash bucket or neighboring buckets, reducing the number of comparisons needed. This approach is particularly effective in large, open environments where objects are sparsely distributed.

Incorporating these efficient data structures into the collision detection pipeline not only enhances performance but also ensures that interactions inside the game world are handled accurately and responsively. The choice of data structure depends on various factors, including the complexity of the environment, the distribution and movement of objects, and the required level of precision. By selecting and implementing the appropriate data structures, developers can optimize collision detection processes, providing players with immersive and believable experiences.

To sum up, efficient data structures play a crucial role in optimizing collision detection in game engines. Spatial partitioning techniques like uniform grids, Quadtrees, and Octrees, hierarchical structures like BVHs and k-DOP trees, and dynamic data structures like sweep and prune and spatial hashing each offer unique advantages in managing the spatial relationships between objects. By leveraging these data structures, developers can achieve both high performance and realistic interactions, ultimately enhancing the overall quality of the game.

Real-Time Collision Response Techniques

In the realm of interactive digital environments, the realism of object interactions is paramount to the immersive experience. One of the key challenges in achieving this realism lies in the effective handling of collision responses. While collision detection identifies when and where objects intersect, collision response determines how these objects should react to these intersections. Real-time collision response techniques are crucial for ensuring that interactions appear natural and believable, maintaining the illusion of a coherent virtual world.

A fundamental aspect of collision response is the calculation of reaction forces and impulses. When two objects collide, they exert forces upon each other, which must be computed to determine their subsequent motions. One common approach is to use impulse-based methods. These methods apply instantaneous changes in velocity to the colliding objects, simulating the effects of the collision. The magnitude and direction of the impulse are determined by the relative velocities and masses of the objects, ensuring that the conservation of momentum and energy laws are respected. This technique is particularly effective for simulating elastic collisions, where objects bounce off each other with minimal energy loss.

Another approach is to employ penalty-based methods. These methods introduce virtual forces that act to separate interpenetrating objects. The forces are proportional to the depth of penetration and act along the direction of the intersection. By applying these corrective forces over multiple simulation steps, the objects are gradually moved apart, resolving the collision. Penalty-based methods are well-suited for simulating soft collisions and interactions involving deformable objects, as they allow for a more controlled and gradual separation process.

Constraint-based techniques also play a significant role in real-time collision response. These techniques enforce specific conditions that must be satisfied during the collision. For example, a constraint might ensure that two objects remain in contact without interpenetrating or slipping past each other. Constraint solvers, such as the Sequential Impulse Solver, are often used to handle these conditions. These solvers iteratively adjust the velocities and positions of the objects to satisfy the constraints, providing stable and realistic responses. Constraint-based methods are particularly effective for handling complex interactions, such as those involving articulated bodies or multi-body systems.

In addition to calculating reaction forces, real-time collision response techniques must also account for friction. Friction is a resistive force that opposes the relative motion of two surfaces in contact. Accurate friction modeling is essential for simulating realistic interactions, as it affects how objects slide, roll, and come to rest. Static friction prevents objects from starting to move, while kinetic friction resists ongoing motion. These forces are typically modeled using coefficients of friction, which determine the strength of the resistive forces based on the normal force and the properties of the surfaces. By incorporating friction into the collision response calculations, developers can ensure that objects behave realistically under various conditions.

Another important consideration is the handling of multiple simultaneous collisions. In dynamic environments, it is common for objects to experience multiple contacts at the same time. This can create complex interaction scenarios that require careful management to ensure stability and realism. One approach is to use contact manifolds, which represent the set of all contact points between two objects. By resolving each contact point individually and then combining the results, the overall collision response can be accurately determined. This technique is particularly useful for handling interactions involving concave surfaces or objects with multiple contact regions.

Continuous collision response is another critical aspect of real-time interaction handling. Traditional collision response methods often operate on discrete time steps, which can lead to issues such as missed collisions or objects passing through each other. Continuous collision response techniques address these issues by tracking the motion of objects over time and ensuring that collisions are detected and resolved continuously. This approach is essential for simulating high-speed interactions and ensuring that objects respond accurately to collisions, regardless of their velocities.

In addition to these core techniques, real-time collision response also involves various optimization strategies to maintain performance. One common optimization is the use of simplified collision shapes, such as bounding boxes or spheres, which reduce the complexity of the collision response calculations. By approximating the true shape of the objects with simpler geometries, the computational load can be significantly reduced, allowing for faster and more efficient simulations. Another optimization is the use of spatial partitioning techniques, which organize the game world into manageable sections and reduce the number of collision checks needed. By focusing computational resources on the most relevant areas, these techniques help maintain real-time performance even in complex environments.

Real-time collision response techniques are also closely integrated with other game systems, such as animation and AI. For example, character animations must be synchronized with the physics engine to ensure that movements appear natural and responsive to collisions. This requires the use of inverse kinematics (IK) systems, which calculate the necessary joint angles to achieve a desired end position while respecting physical constraints. Similarly, AI systems must consider physical interactions when planning and executing actions, such as navigating obstacles or engaging in combat. By integrating collision response techniques with these systems, developers can create cohesive and immersive experiences that respond authentically to player actions.

To sum it all up, real-time collision response techniques are essential for ensuring realistic interactions in interactive digital environments. By employing impulse-based methods, penalty-based methods, constraint-based techniques, and friction modeling, developers can achieve natural and believable responses to collisions. Additionally, handling multiple simultaneous collisions, continuous collision response, and various optimization strategies are crucial for maintaining performance and realism. By integrating these techniques with other game systems, developers can create immersive and dynamic experiences that captivate players and bring virtual worlds to life.

Optimizing Performance in Collision Handling

In the intricate domain of game development, the efficiency and realism of object interactions are paramount. Ensuring that virtual elements respond to collisions in a convincing manner while maintaining optimal performance is a sophisticated challenge. This section delves into the strategies and methodologies employed to enhance the performance of collision handling inside game engines, ensuring that interactions remain both realistic and computationally efficient.

One of the foundational strategies for optimizing collision performance is the use of spatial partitioning. This technique involves dividing the game world into smaller, manageable sections, thereby reducing the number of collision checks needed. By organizing objects into predefined areas, the collision detection algorithm can quickly identify which objects are likely to intersect. A common method for spatial partitioning is the use of grids, where the game space is divided into a network of cells. Objects are assigned to these cells based on their positions, and collision checks are limited to objects inside the same or neighboring cells. This significantly reduces the computational load, especially in large and densely populated environments.

Another advanced approach to spatial partitioning is the implementation of hierarchical data structures. Techniques such as Quadtrees and Octrees are particularly effective in managing varying object densities and dynamic environments. Quadtrees recursively subdivide a two-dimensional space, while Octrees extend this concept to three dimensions. These hierarchical structures allow for adaptive partitioning, where regions with higher object densities are further subdivided. This adaptability ensures that computational resources are focused on areas with more potential collisions, thereby enhancing overall performance.

Bounding volume hierarchies (BVH) offer another powerful method for optimizing collision handling. BVHs organize objects into a tree of nested bounding volumes, each encapsulating a group of objects or sub-volumes. This hierarchical approach enables quick exclusion of large sets of non-colliding objects, reducing the number of detailed collision checks required. By traversing the hierarchy from the root to the leaves, the collision detection algorithm can efficiently focus on intersecting volumes, making BVHs highly effective for scenes with numerous objects.

In addition to hierarchical structures, the use of simplified collision shapes can significantly enhance performance. Simplified shapes, such as spheres, capsules, and axis-aligned bounding boxes, provide approximate representations of objects, reducing the complexity of collision calculations. For instance, a complex model of a character can be approximated by a capsule shape for collision purposes. While this approach may sacrifice some accuracy, it offers substantial gains in computational efficiency, making it suitable for real-time applications where performance is critical.

Dynamic environments, where objects frequently move and interact, present unique challenges for collision handling. To address these challenges, dynamic data structures such as the sweep and prune algorithm are employed. This method involves sorting objects along one or more axes and then checking for overlapping intervals. As objects move, the sorted order is updated, allowing for efficient identification of potential collisions. Sweep and prune is particularly advantageous in scenarios with frequent object movements, as it maintains an up-to-date list of potential collisions with minimal computational overhead.

Another dynamic data structure that enhances collision performance is the spatial hash. Spatial hashing maps objects to a hash table based on their positions, enabling quick insertion, deletion, and querying. When checking for collisions, the algorithm only needs to consider objects inside the same hash bucket or neighboring buckets, reducing the number of comparisons. Spatial hashing is especially effective in large, open environments where objects are sparsely distributed, providing a balance between accuracy and performance.

Efficient collision handling also involves optimizing the algorithms used to detect collisions. One such optimization is the use of broad-phase and narrow-phase collision detection. Broad-phase algorithms quickly eliminate pairs of objects that are unlikely to collide, reducing the number of pairs that need detailed checks. Techniques such as sweep and prune, grid-based methods, and hierarchical structures are commonly used in the broad phase. Once potential collisions are identified, narrow-phase algorithms perform precise calculations to determine the exact points of intersection. This two-phase approach ensures that computational resources are allocated efficiently, focusing detailed checks only on likely collisions.

To further enhance performance, continuous collision detection (CCD) techniques are employed. Traditional collision detection methods often operate on discrete time steps, which can lead to missed collisions or objects passing through each other. CCD addresses these issues by tracking the motion of objects over time, ensuring that collisions are detected and resolved continuously. This approach is essential for simulating high-speed interactions and maintaining accuracy, regardless of object velocities.

Another critical aspect of optimizing collision handling is the integration of predictive algorithms. Predictive algorithms anticipate potential collisions based on the current trajectories of objects, allowing the collision detection system to preemptively manage interactions. By forecasting future collisions, these algorithms can reduce the frequency and complexity of real-time collision checks, enhancing overall performance. Predictive collision handling is particularly useful in scenarios involving fast-moving objects or complex interactions, where timely responses are crucial.

Parallel processing is another powerful optimization technique for collision handling. By leveraging multi-core processors and graphics processing units (GPUs), collision detection and response calculations can be distributed across multiple threads. This parallelization allows for simultaneous processing of multiple collision checks, significantly reducing the overall computation time. Modern game engines often implement parallel processing to handle the intensive demands of collision handling, ensuring that performance remains high even in complex environments.

In addition to these strategies, real-time performance profiling and optimization tools play a vital role in collision handling. Profiling tools allow developers to identify performance bottlenecks and optimize specific aspects of the collision detection pipeline. By analyzing frame rates, CPU and GPU usage, and memory consumption, developers can fine-tune algorithms and data structures to achieve optimal performance. Continuous profiling and optimization are essential for maintaining high performance, especially as game environments and interactions evolve during development.

To summarize, optimizing performance in collision handling is a multifaceted challenge that requires a combination of advanced techniques and methodologies. Spatial partitioning, hierarchical data structures, simplified collision shapes, dynamic data structures, broad-phase and narrow-phase algorithms, continuous collision detection, predictive algorithms, parallel processing, and real-time profiling all contribute to enhancing the efficiency and realism of collision handling in game engines. By implementing these strategies, developers can ensure that interactions inside the virtual world are both convincing and computationally efficient, providing players with immersive and responsive experiences.

Advanced Collision Detection Methods and Innovations

In the evolving landscape of interactive digital environments, the quest for lifelike object interactions necessitates the continuous advancement of collision detection techniques. As game worlds grow more complex and visually rich, the methods used to identify and manage collisions must also evolve. This section delves into the sophisticated techniques and innovative approaches that are pushing the boundaries of collision detection, ensuring that interactions inside virtual spaces are both realistic and computationally efficient.

One of the cutting-edge methods in collision detection involves the use of machine learning algorithms. These algorithms can be trained to predict potential collisions based on historical data and patterns observed in gameplay. By analyzing vast amounts of interaction data, machine learning models can identify subtle cues that might indicate an impending collision, allowing the game engine to preemptively manage interactions. This predictive capability not only enhances the realism of the game but also reduces the computational load by focusing resources on the most likely collision scenarios.

Another innovative approach is the utilization of hybrid collision detection systems. These systems combine multiple detection techniques to leverage their respective strengths. For instance, a hybrid system might use a broad-phase method for initial collision screening, followed by a more precise narrow-phase method for detailed intersection analysis. By dynamically switching between different techniques based on the context and requirements of the game, hybrid systems can achieve a balance between accuracy and performance. This adaptability is particularly beneficial in dynamic environments where the nature of interactions can vary widely.

The integration of procedural generation with collision detection presents another frontier of innovation. Procedural generation techniques create game content algorithmically, allowing for vast and varied environments. Incorporating collision detection into this process ensures that generated content is not only visually appealing but also interactively coherent. For example, a procedurally generated landscape might include naturally occurring obstacles and pathways, with collision detection algorithms ensuring that these elements interact realistically with player movements. This seamless integration enhances both the immersion and the unpredictability of the game world.

In virtual and augmented reality, advanced collision detection methods are crucial for maintaining the illusion of presence. Techniques such as ray tracing and voxel-based collision detection are increasingly being employed to manage interactions in these immersive environments. Ray tracing involves tracing the path of light rays to detect intersections with objects, providing highly accurate collision data. Voxel-based methods, on the other hand, represent the game world as a grid of volumetric pixels (voxels), allowing for precise detection of collisions at a granular level. These techniques are particularly effective in VR and AR applications, where the fidelity of interactions directly impacts the user's sense of immersion.

The advent of multi-threaded processing and parallel computation has also revolutionized collision detection. By distributing collision calculations across multiple processing cores or even utilizing the parallel processing capabilities of GPUs, game engines can handle more complex interactions without compromising performance. This parallelization allows for simultaneous processing of multiple collision checks, significantly reducing the overall computation time. As a result, games can feature more intricate interactions and larger numbers of dynamic objects, all while maintaining smooth and responsive gameplay.

Another area of innovation is the development of adaptive collision detection algorithms. These algorithms adjust their level of detail and precision based on the current state of the game. For instance, interactions that occur near the player's focus might be handled with high precision, while those in peripheral areas might use more approximate methods. This adaptive approach ensures that computational resources are allocated efficiently, prioritizing the most critical interactions. Additionally, adaptive algorithms can dynamically adjust their parameters based on real-time performance metrics, ensuring a consistent experience even as the complexity of the game world fluctuates.

The use of physics-based animation in conjunction with collision detection is another advanced technique gaining traction. Physics-based animation systems simulate the physical properties of objects, allowing for realistic movements and interactions. When integrated with collision detection, these systems can produce highly believable responses to collisions. For example, a character might realistically stumble and recover after colliding with an obstacle, with the movements driven by simulated forces and constraints. This integration enhances the believability of interactions, making them appear more natural and spontaneous.

Innovations in sensor technology and input devices are also influencing collision detection methods. Devices such as motion capture systems and depth-sensing cameras provide detailed data about the physical movements of players, which can be used to enhance collision detection accuracy. For instance, a motion capture system might track a player's hand movements, allowing for precise detection of interactions with virtual objects. Similarly, depth-sensing cameras can create a 3D map of the player's environment, enabling the game engine to account for real-world obstacles and interactions. These advancements are particularly relevant in mixed reality applications, where the boundary between the virtual and physical worlds is increasingly blurred.

Finally, the exploration of quantum computing holds potential for future advancements in collision detection. Quantum computers can process vast amounts of data simultaneously, offering unprecedented computational power. While still in the experimental stage, quantum algorithms could revolutionize collision detection by enabling real-time analysis of extremely complex interactions. This potential could lead to game worlds with unparalleled levels of detail and interactivity, pushing the boundaries of what is currently possible.

In summary, the field of collision detection is witnessing significant advancements driven by machine learning, hybrid systems, procedural generation, virtual and augmented reality, parallel computation, adaptive algorithms, physics-based animation, sensor technology, and the emerging potential of quantum computing. These innovations are not only enhancing the realism of interactions inside game worlds but also ensuring that these interactions are managed efficiently. As technology continues to evolve, the methods used to detect and respond to collisions will undoubtedly become even more sophisticated, further blurring the line between virtual and real-world experiences.

Fluid Dynamics: Simulating Liquids And Gases

Fundamentals of Fluid Dynamics in Game Engines

Fluid dynamics plays a pivotal role in crafting engaging and realistic virtual worlds. Simulating the behavior of liquids and gases inside a digital environment involves intricate processes that require both theoretical understanding and practical implementation. In this section, we will explore the foundational concepts underpinning fluid dynamics in game engines, examining how these principles are applied to create believable simulations.

To begin with, fluid dynamics is governed by a set of fundamental principles, primarily derived from the Navier-Stokes equations. These equations describe the motion of fluid substances by considering factors such as velocity, pressure, density, and viscosity. Understanding these parameters is crucial for developers aiming to implement accurate fluid simulations. The Navier-Stokes equations can be computationally intensive, often necessitating the use of numerical methods and algorithms to achieve real-time performance in game engines.

One of the key challenges in fluid dynamics simulation is the representation of continuous fluid flow inside a discrete computational space. This is typically addressed through techniques such as the Eulerian and Lagrangian methods. The Eulerian method involves dividing the simulation space into a grid, where fluid properties are calculated at fixed points. This approach is advantageous for handling large-scale simulations, such as ocean waves or atmospheric phenomena. On the other hand, the Lagrangian method tracks individual fluid particles as they move through space, which is particularly useful for simulating smaller-scale effects like splashes or smoke.

In addition to these methods, hybrid approaches combine the strengths of both Eulerian and Lagrangian techniques to achieve more versatile simulations. For instance, the Particle-In-Cell (PIC) method uses a grid-based approach to handle fluid properties while tracking particles to capture fine details. This allows for a balance between computational efficiency and simulation accuracy, making it a popular choice for game engine developers.

Another critical aspect of fluid dynamics in game engines is the handling of boundary conditions. Fluids interact with various surfaces and objects inside the game environment, and accurately modeling these interactions is essential for realism. Techniques such as level set methods and ghost fluid methods are employed to manage the interface between fluids and solid boundaries. These techniques ensure that fluid behavior is consistent with physical laws, providing a more immersive experience for players.

Moreover, the simulation of fluid dynamics often requires the integration of additional physical phenomena, such as turbulence and buoyancy. Turbulence, characterized by chaotic and irregular fluid motion, is particularly challenging to simulate due to its complex nature. Developers employ methods like the Reynolds-Averaged Navier-Stokes (RANS) equations or Large Eddy Simulation (LES) to approximate turbulent flows. Buoyancy, which describes the upward force exerted on objects submerged in a fluid, is another important factor that influences fluid behavior. Incorporating these effects into simulations enhances the realism and interactivity of the game environment.

The computational demands of fluid dynamics simulations necessitate the use of optimization techniques to achieve real-time performance. One common approach is to simplify the simulation by reducing the resolution of the computational grid or the number of particles. While this can improve performance, it may also lead to a loss of detail. Developers must strike a balance between performance and visual fidelity, often employing techniques such as adaptive mesh refinement, where the resolution is dynamically adjusted based on the complexity of the fluid motion.

Furthermore, advancements in hardware and parallel computing have significantly impacted the field of fluid dynamics in game engines. Graphics Processing Units (GPUs) are particularly well-suited for the parallel nature of fluid simulations, allowing for substantial performance improvements. By leveraging GPU acceleration, developers can achieve more detailed and realistic fluid simulations without compromising on real-time interactivity.

To sum it all up, the fundamentals of fluid dynamics in game engines encompass a wide range of principles and techniques, each contributing to the creation of immersive and believable virtual worlds. From the mathematical foundations of the Navier-Stokes equations to the practical implementation of numerical methods and optimization techniques, understanding these elements is essential for any developer aiming to simulate liquids and gases effectively. As hardware capabilities continue to evolve, the potential for even more sophisticated fluid dynamics simulations in game engines will undoubtedly expand, offering exciting possibilities for the future of interactive entertainment.

Navier-Stokes Equations: Governing Fluid Motion

In game development, simulating the motion of fluids—both liquids and gases—requires a robust understanding of the underlying physical principles that govern their behavior. Central to this understanding are the Navier-Stokes equations, a set of partial differential equations that describe how the velocity field of a fluid evolves over time. These equations are foundational in fluid dynamics and are essential for developers aiming to create realistic and interactive fluid simulations in game engines.

The Navier-Stokes equations encompass several key variables: velocity, pressure, density, and viscosity, each contributing to the overall fluid behavior in unique ways. Velocity represents the speed and direction of fluid particles, while pressure denotes the force exerted by the fluid per unit area. Density is a measure of the fluid's mass per unit volume, and viscosity quantifies the fluid's internal resistance to flow. Together, these variables form a comprehensive framework for modeling fluid motion.

At their core, the Navier-Stokes equations consist of the continuity equation and the momentum equation. The continuity equation ensures mass conservation inside the fluid, stating that the rate of change of fluid density inside a volume is equal to the net flux of fluid across the boundary of that volume. Mathematically, this is expressed as:

$$\partial \rho / \partial t + \nabla \cdot (\rho u) = 0$$

Where ρ represents the fluid density, u is the velocity vector, and $\nabla \cdot (\rho u)$ denotes the divergence of the mass flux.

The momentum equation, on the other hand, is derived from Newton's second law and accounts for the forces acting on the fluid. It is expressed as:

$$\rho(\partial u/\partial t + u \cdot \nabla u) = -\nabla p + \mu \nabla^2 u + f$$

In this equation, $\partial u/\partial t$ represents the rate of change of velocity, $u \cdot \nabla u$ is the convective term describing the change in velocity due to the fluid's motion, $-\nabla p$ is the pressure gradient force, $\mu \nabla^2 u$ is the viscous term accounting for internal friction, and f denotes any external forces acting on the fluid, such as gravity.

Solving the Navier-Stokes equations analytically is often impractical due to their nonlinearity and the complexity of real-world fluid interactions. Instead, numerical methods are employed to approximate solutions. One common approach is the finite difference method, which discretizes the fluid domain into a grid and approximates the differential operators using finite differences. This method is particularly useful for structured grids and can provide accurate results for a wide range of fluid flow scenarios.

Another popular technique is the finite volume method, which divides the fluid domain into control volumes and applies the conservation laws to each volume. This approach ensures conservation properties are maintained across the entire domain and is well-suited for unstructured grids, making it versatile for complex geometries.

The finite element method, meanwhile, represents the fluid domain using a mesh of elements and approximates the solution using basis functions. This method is highly flexible and can handle irregular geometries and boundary conditions with ease. It is particularly effective for simulating fluid-structure interactions, where the fluid interacts with deformable or moving boundaries.

In game engine development, achieving real-time performance is crucial. As such, developers often employ simplified models or hybrid methods to balance accuracy and computational efficiency. One such method is the lattice Boltzmann method, which models fluid dynamics using a discrete lattice grid and particle collision rules. This method can capture complex flow phenomena with relatively low computational cost, making it suitable for real-time applications.

Boundary conditions play a significant role in fluid simulations, as they define how the fluid interacts with the environment. Common boundary conditions include no-slip conditions, where the fluid velocity at a solid boundary is zero, and free-slip conditions, where the fluid can move tangentially along the boundary without friction. Implementing accurate boundary conditions is essential for ensuring realistic fluid behavior, particularly in scenarios involving fluid-solid interactions or open boundaries.

Turbulence, a phenomenon characterized by chaotic and irregular fluid motion, presents a significant challenge in fluid simulations. To address this, developers often use turbulence models such as the Reynolds-Averaged Navier-Stokes (RANS) equations, which average the effects of turbulence over time, or Large Eddy Simulation (LES), which resolves larger turbulent structures while modeling smaller ones. These models provide a balance between computational efficiency and the ability to capture essential turbulent features.

In addition to traditional numerical methods, advancements in machine learning have opened new avenues for fluid simulation. Neural networks and deep learning algorithms can be trained to predict fluid behavior based on data from high-fidelity simulations. These data-driven approaches can offer significant speedups while maintaining a high level of accuracy, making them promising tools for real-time applications.

The integration of hardware acceleration, particularly through Graphics Processing Units (GPUs), has further revolutionized fluid simulations. GPUs are well-suited for the parallel nature of fluid computations, enabling developers to achieve substantial performance gains. By leveraging GPU acceleration, it is possible to perform complex fluid simulations at interactive frame rates, enhancing the realism and interactivity of game environments.

To summarize, the Navier-Stokes equations serve as the cornerstone of fluid dynamics, providing a comprehensive framework for modeling fluid motion. While solving these equations analytically is often infeasible, numerical methods and computational techniques offer practical solutions for simulating fluids in game engines. By understanding the principles and challenges associated with the Navier-Stokes equations, developers can create realistic and engaging fluid simulations that enhance the immersive experience of virtual worlds. As technology continues to advance, the potential for even more sophisticated and efficient fluid simulations will undoubtedly expand, offering exciting possibilities for the future of game development.

Particle-Based Methods for Fluid Simulation

In fluid simulation, particle-based methods have carved a niche due to their flexibility and adaptability in handling complex fluid behaviors. These methods focus on representing fluids through discrete particles, each carrying properties like position, velocity, and mass. Unlike grid-based approaches, particle-based techniques offer a more intuitive way to simulate fluid interactions, especially in dynamic and deformable environments. This section delves into the principles, advantages, and practical implementations of particle-based methods in fluid simulation, providing a comprehensive understanding of their role in creating convincing virtual worlds.

At the core of particle-based fluid simulation lies the concept of representing a fluid as a collection of particles. Each particle acts as a carrier of fluid properties, allowing the simulation to track the motion and interaction of individual fluid elements. This approach offers significant advantages when dealing with complex geometries and free-surface flows, where traditional grid-based methods may struggle. By treating fluids as particles, developers can more easily model phenomena such as splashes, sprays, and turbulent flows.

One of the most widely used particle-based methods is Smoothed Particle Hydrodynamics (SPH). SPH was initially developed for astrophysical simulations but has since found extensive applications in computer graphics and game development. In SPH, each particle carries properties such as density, velocity, and pressure, which are computed based on the contributions of neighboring particles. The interactions between particles are governed by smoothing kernels, mathematical functions that define the influence radius of each particle. These kernels ensure smooth transitions between particle properties, thereby providing a continuous representation of the fluid.

The SPH method operates by solving the equations of fluid motion in a Lagrangian framework, where the focus is on individual particles as they move through space. This is in contrast to Eulerian methods, which compute fluid properties at fixed grid points. The Lagrangian nature of SPH allows it to naturally handle complex boundary conditions and free surfaces, making it well-suited for simulating phenomena such as breaking waves, splashing water, and flowing rivers.

To simulate fluid behavior using SPH, several key steps are involved. First, the fluid domain is populated with particles, each assigned initial properties such as position, velocity, and mass. The density of each particle is then computed by summing the contributions of neighboring particles inside a specified radius. This density is used to calculate the pressure forces acting on each particle, which in turn influence their acceleration and velocity. The positions of the particles are updated based on their velocities, completing the simulation loop.

While SPH offers a robust framework for fluid simulation, it is not without challenges. One of the primary difficulties lies in maintaining stability and preventing numerical artifacts, such as particle clumping or excessive diffusion. Various techniques have been developed to address these issues, including the use of artificial viscosity to dampen high-frequency oscillations and the incorporation of surface tension models to capture the cohesive forces between fluid particles.

Another particle-based method worth mentioning is the Position-Based Fluids (PBF) approach. PBF, as the name suggests, focuses on directly manipulating the positions of particles to enforce fluid constraints. This method is particularly popular in real-time applications, such as video games, due to its computational efficiency and stability. In PBF, fluid particles are iteratively adjusted to satisfy constraints related to density, boundary conditions, and fluid incompressibility. By solving these constraints in a position-based framework, PBF can achieve stable and visually plausible fluid simulations even at low computational costs.

In addition to SPH and PBF, other particle-based techniques have been explored for fluid simulation. One such method is the Moving Particle Semi-implicit (MPS) approach, which combines the advantages of particle-based and grid-based methods. MPS uses particles to represent the fluid but employs a semi-implicit integration scheme to enhance stability and accuracy. This hybrid approach allows MPS to handle complex fluid interactions and boundary conditions effectively, making it a versatile tool for fluid simulation in game engines.

The practical implementation of particle-based fluid simulation involves several considerations, including particle initialization, neighbor search algorithms, and parallelization techniques. Initializing particles uniformly inside the fluid domain is crucial for maintaining a consistent simulation. Neighbor search algorithms, such as spatial hashing or k-d trees, are employed to efficiently identify neighboring particles inside a specified radius. Parallelization techniques, leveraging multi-core CPUs or GPUs, are essential for achieving real-time performance in particle-based simulations.

One of the key advantages of particle-based methods is their ability to handle complex fluid interactions with solid objects. In game engines, this capability is essential for creating realistic interactions between fluids and characters, terrain, or other dynamic objects. By treating solid boundaries as collections of particles or using boundary handling techniques, particle-based methods can simulate fluid-solid interactions with high fidelity. This enables developers to create immersive experiences, such as characters wading through water, objects floating and sinking, or fluids flowing around obstacles.

Moreover, particle-based methods offer a natural framework for simulating multiphase flows, where different fluid phases coexist and interact. For instance, simulating the interaction between water and air, or oil and water, can be challenging using traditional grid-based methods. Particle-based techniques, however, can seamlessly handle the mixing and separation of different fluid phases, allowing for the creation of visually stunning effects such as foam, bubbles, and emulsions.

In recent years, advancements in hardware and software have further enhanced the capabilities of particle-based fluid simulation. The advent of powerful GPUs has enabled the development of highly parallelizable algorithms, significantly accelerating the computation of particle interactions. Additionally, advancements in machine learning and data-driven approaches have opened new avenues for improving the accuracy and efficiency of particle-based simulations. By training neural networks on high-fidelity simulation data, developers can create predictive models that approximate fluid behavior with remarkable speed and precision.

Essentially, particle-based methods have emerged as a powerful tool for simulating fluids in game engines. Their flexibility, adaptability, and ability to handle complex fluid interactions make them an invaluable asset for developers seeking to create realistic and immersive virtual environments. From the foundational principles of SPH and PBF to the practical considerations of implementation and optimization, understanding particle-based fluid simulation is essential for pushing the boundaries of what is possible in interactive entertainment. As technology continues to evolve, particle-based methods will undoubtedly play a pivotal role in shaping the future of fluid simulation in game development.

Grid-Based Techniques for Simulating Fluids

Grid-based techniques are fundamental to simulating fluid behavior in digital environments. These approaches rely on discretizing the fluid domain into a structured grid, where fluid properties are computed at fixed grid points. This method offers a structured and systematic way to handle the complexities inherent in fluid simulations, making it a popular choice among developers and researchers. In this section, we will explore the foundational principles, various grid-based methods, and practical considerations for implementing these techniques in game engines.

One of the primary advantages of grid-based techniques is their ability to efficiently handle large-scale fluid simulations. By dividing the simulation space into a grid, developers can systematically compute fluid properties such as velocity, pressure, and density at each grid cell. This structured approach simplifies the process of solving the governing equations of fluid motion, enabling accurate and stable simulations.

A widely used grid-based method is the finite difference method (FDM). FDM involves approximating the derivatives in the governing equations using finite differences, which are computed based on the values of fluid properties at adjacent grid points. This method is particularly effective for structured grids, where the grid cells are uniformly spaced. By discretizing the fluid domain into a grid, FDM transforms the continuous equations into a system of algebraic equations that can be solved iteratively.

Another prominent grid-based technique is the finite volume method (FVM). Unlike FDM, which focuses on approximating derivatives, FVM emphasizes the conservation laws of fluid motion. In FVM, the fluid domain is divided into control volumes, and the governing equations are integrated over each control volume. This approach ensures that conservation properties, such as mass and momentum, are maintained across the entire domain. FVM is particularly versatile and can handle unstructured grids, making it suitable for complex geometries.

The finite element method (FEM) is another powerful grid-based technique used in fluid simulations. FEM represents the fluid domain using a mesh of elements, and the governing equations are approximated using basis functions defined over these elements. This method is highly flexible and can handle irregular geometries and boundary conditions with ease. FEM is particularly effective for simulating fluid-structure interactions, where the fluid interacts with deformable or moving boundaries.

In addition to these traditional grid-based methods, the lattice Boltzmann method (LBM) has gained popularity in recent years. LBM models fluid dynamics using a discrete lattice grid and particle collision rules. This method captures complex flow phenomena with relatively low computational cost, making it suitable for real-time applications. LBM operates by tracking the distribution of particle velocities at each lattice point and updating these distributions based on collision and streaming processes. This approach allows LBM to simulate fluid motion efficiently while maintaining a high level of accuracy.

One of the key challenges in grid-based fluid simulations is handling boundary conditions. Boundary conditions define how the fluid interacts with the environment, such as solid boundaries or open boundaries. Implementing accurate boundary conditions is crucial for ensuring realistic fluid behavior. Common boundary conditions include no-slip conditions, where the fluid velocity at a solid boundary is zero, and free-slip conditions, where the fluid can move tangentially along the boundary without friction. Techniques such as ghost cells and immersed boundary methods are employed to handle complex boundary interactions.

Grid-based techniques also require careful consideration of numerical stability and accuracy. The Courant-Friedrichs-Lewy (CFL) condition is a critical criterion for ensuring stability in fluid simulations. The CFL condition states that the time step used in the simulation must be small enough to ensure that the fluid properties do not change too rapidly between grid points. Violating the CFL condition can lead to numerical instabilities and inaccurate results. Developers often employ adaptive time-stepping algorithms to dynamically adjust the time step based on the fluid motion.

Another important aspect of grid-based fluid simulations is the resolution of the computational grid. Higher grid resolutions provide more detailed and accurate simulations but come at the cost of increased computational resources. Developers must strike a balance between resolution and performance, often employing techniques such as adaptive mesh refinement (AMR). AMR dynamically adjusts the grid resolution based on the complexity of the fluid motion, allowing for efficient simulations without sacrificing accuracy.

Parallel computing plays a significant role in enhancing the performance of grid-based fluid simulations. By distributing the computation across multiple processors or using Graphics Processing Units (GPUs), developers can achieve substantial speedups. Parallel algorithms, such as domain decomposition and multi-grid methods, are employed to efficiently distribute the computational workload. Leveraging parallel computing enables real-time fluid simulations, enhancing the interactivity and realism of game environments.

Grid-based techniques also offer a natural framework for simulating multiphase flows, where different fluid phases coexist and interact. For instance, simulating the interaction between water and air, or oil and water, can be challenging using other methods. Grid-based techniques can handle the mixing and separation of different fluid phases, allowing for the creation of visually stunning effects such as splashes, bubbles, and emulsions. Volume of fluid (VOF) and level set methods are commonly used to track the interfaces between different fluid phases in grid-based simulations.

In recent years, advancements in machine learning have opened new possibilities for grid-based fluid simulations. Neural networks and deep learning algorithms can be trained to predict fluid behavior based on data from high-fidelity simulations. These data-driven approaches offer significant speedups while maintaining a high level of accuracy, making them promising tools for real-time applications. By incorporating machine learning techniques, developers can enhance the efficiency and realism of grid-based fluid simulations.

To finalize, grid-based techniques are essential for simulating fluid behavior in game engines. From the finite difference method to the lattice Boltzmann method, each approach offers unique advantages and challenges. By understanding the principles and practical considerations of grid-based techniques, developers can create realistic and immersive fluid simulations that enhance the interactive experience of virtual worlds. As technology continues to evolve, the potential for even more sophisticated and efficient grid-based fluid simulations will undoubtedly expand, offering exciting possibilities for the future of game development.

Hybrid Approaches in Fluid Simulation

Fluid simulation is a cornerstone in the development of interactive and realistic virtual environments. Traditional methods, while robust, often encounter limitations in balancing accuracy and computational efficiency. This has led to the exploration and adoption of hybrid approaches, which combine multiple techniques to leverage their individual strengths and mitigate weaknesses. Hybrid approaches in fluid simulation offer a versatile and efficient framework, enabling developers to achieve high fidelity simulations without compromising performance.

Hybrid methods typically integrate aspects of both particle-based and grid-based techniques, allowing for a more flexible and adaptive simulation environment. By combining these methodologies, developers can harness the advantages of each, such as the detailed local interactions offered by particle-based approaches and the global consistency provided by grid-based methods. This synergy facilitates the creation of complex fluid behaviors that are computationally feasible for real-time applications.

One prominent hybrid approach is the Particle-in-Cell (PIC) method. PIC combines the Lagrangian perspective of particle-based methods with the Eulerian framework of grid-based techniques. In PIC, particles carry fluid properties like mass and momentum, while the grid provides a structured domain for solving the governing equations of fluid motion. The particles are used to interpolate fluid quantities onto the grid, where the equations are solved. The updated grid values are then interpolated back to the particles. This bidirectional exchange ensures both local detail and global coherence, making PIC suitable for simulating intricate fluid phenomena.

An extension of PIC is the Fluid-Implicit Particle (FLIP) method, which addresses some of the numerical dissipation issues inherent in PIC. FLIP retains the advantages of PIC but incorporates a correction step that reduces the smoothing of particle velocities during grid interpolation. This results in a more accurate representation of fluid motion, particularly in scenarios involving high-energy interactions like splashes or turbulence. By maintaining the benefits of both particle and grid-based methods, FLIP achieves a balance between fidelity and computational efficiency.

Another hybrid technique is the Adaptive Mesh Particle Simulation (AMPS), which dynamically adjusts the resolution of the computational grid based on the complexity of the fluid motion. In AMPS, a coarse grid is used for regions with relatively smooth fluid behavior, while finer grids are applied to areas with intricate dynamics. Particles are employed to track fluid properties and ensure detailed interactions. This adaptive approach minimizes computational overhead by concentrating resources where they are needed most, enabling real-time performance without sacrificing accuracy.

Hybrid approaches also extend to the use of level set methods combined with particles for interface tracking. Level set methods represent fluid interfaces implicitly through a signed distance function, which evolves over time to capture the fluid's shape. By coupling this with particles that carry additional information about the interface, developers can achieve a more precise and stable representation of fluid boundaries. This combination is particularly effective for simulating scenarios where the fluid interface undergoes significant deformation or fragmentation, such as breaking waves or splashing liquids.

Incorporating machine learning into hybrid fluid simulation has opened new avenues for enhancing both performance and realism. Neural networks can be trained on high-fidelity simulation data to predict fluid behavior, effectively acting as surrogate models that approximate complex fluid dynamics. These data-driven models can be integrated with traditional simulation techniques to accelerate computations while maintaining a high level of detail. For instance, a neural network might predict the coarse behavior of a fluid, while a particle-based method refines the local interactions. This hybrid approach leverages the predictive power of machine learning and the precision of traditional methods, offering a promising path for real-time fluid simulation.

The integration of hardware acceleration, particularly through Graphics Processing Units (GPUs), plays a crucial role in the feasibility of hybrid approaches. GPUs are well-suited for the parallel nature of fluid computations, enabling significant speedups. Hybrid methods can be optimized to exploit GPU architecture, distributing tasks such as particle advection, grid-based computations, and interpolation efficiently across multiple cores. This parallelization is essential for achieving interactive frame rates in complex simulations, enhancing the immersive quality of virtual environments.

Boundary conditions are a critical aspect of fluid simulation, and hybrid approaches offer unique advantages in handling them. By combining particle and grid-based methods, developers can implement more accurate and flexible boundary interactions. For example, solid boundaries can be represented using particles that interact with the fluid, while the grid ensures global consistency of the fluid motion. This dual representation allows for more realistic simulations of fluid-solid interactions, such as water flowing around obstacles or objects floating and sinking.

Turbulence modeling is another area where hybrid techniques excel. Traditional turbulence models often struggle with the trade-off between accuracy and computational cost. Hybrid approaches can address this by using particles to capture small-scale turbulent structures and a grid to model the larger flow dynamics. This multi-scale representation provides a more comprehensive depiction of turbulence, enhancing the realism of fluid simulations in scenarios like smoke, fire, or fast-moving fluids.

The versatility of hybrid approaches extends to multiphase flow simulations, where different fluid phases coexist and interact. By combining particle-based methods for tracking individual phases with grid-based techniques for solving the overall flow, developers can achieve a detailed and accurate representation of multiphase interactions. This is particularly useful for simulating complex phenomena such as oil-water separation, bubble formation, or the mixing of different liquids.

In summary, hybrid approaches in fluid simulation represent a powerful and flexible framework for achieving high-fidelity and efficient simulations. By integrating particle-based and grid-based methods, leveraging machine learning, and optimizing for hardware acceleration, developers can push the boundaries of what is possible in real-time fluid simulation. These techniques offer a balanced solution to the challenges of simulating complex fluid behaviors, enabling the creation of more immersive and interactive virtual environments. As technology continues to advance, hybrid approaches will undoubtedly play a pivotal role in the future of fluid simulation in game development.

Real-Time Rendering of Liquids and Gases

Rendering fluids, whether liquids or gases, in real-time is a captivating challenge that blends the art of visual aesthetics with the science of computational physics. This section delves into the techniques and methodologies employed to achieve realistic and interactive fluid simulations in game engines. By examining various aspects of fluid rendering, we can appreciate the intricate balance between computational efficiency and visual fidelity that defines state-of-the-art fluid simulations.

One of the primary goals in real-time fluid rendering is to create visually convincing simulations that respond dynamically to user interactions and environmental changes. This requires a seamless integration of physical simulation and graphical representation. The process begins with the accurate simulation of fluid behavior, which involves solving the governing equations of fluid dynamics. These equations describe how fluids move and interact with their surroundings, capturing phenomena such as flow, turbulence, and viscosity.

To achieve real-time performance, developers often employ simplified models and approximations that strike a balance between detail and computational cost. One common approach is to use particle systems to represent fluids. In this method, fluids are modeled as a collection of discrete particles, each carrying properties such as position, velocity, and color. Particle systems are particularly effective for simulating free-flowing liquids and gases, as they can easily adapt to changing shapes and boundaries.

In addition to particle systems, grid-based methods are frequently used in real-time fluid rendering. These methods discretize the fluid domain into a structured grid, where fluid properties are computed at fixed grid points. Grid-based methods are well-suited for capturing large-scale fluid behaviors and ensuring global consistency in the simulation. Techniques such as the finite difference method and the finite volume method are commonly employed to solve the fluid equations on the grid.

One of the key challenges in real-time fluid rendering is handling the complex interactions between fluids and solid objects. This is particularly important in game environments, where fluids often encounter characters, terrain, and other dynamic elements. To address this, developers use techniques such as boundary handling and collision detection. Boundary handling ensures that fluids respect the boundaries of solid objects, while collision detection identifies and responds to interactions between fluids and solids.

Another critical aspect of real-time fluid rendering is the visualization of fluid surfaces. For liquids, this involves generating a smooth and continuous surface that accurately represents the shape and motion of the fluid. Techniques such as surface reconstruction and mesh generation are employed to create a visually appealing fluid surface. Surface reconstruction methods use the positions of fluid particles to generate a continuous surface, often through techniques like marching cubes or level set methods. Mesh generation then converts this surface into a polygonal mesh that can be rendered by the graphics engine.

For gases, the visualization process focuses on capturing the diffuse and dynamic nature of gaseous flows. Volume rendering techniques are commonly used to achieve this. Volume rendering involves representing the gas as a three-dimensional volume, where properties such as density and temperature are stored at each voxel (volumetric pixel). The rendering process then involves computing the light interaction with the gas volume, often using techniques such as ray marching or splatting. These techniques create the appearance of light scattering and absorption inside the gas, resulting in realistic visual effects such as smoke, fog, and fire.

Lighting and shading play a crucial role in enhancing the realism of fluid simulations. Accurate lighting models are essential for capturing the way light interacts with fluid surfaces and volumes. For liquids, reflection and refraction effects are particularly important. Techniques such as screen-space reflections and refraction mapping are used to simulate these effects in real-time. Screen-space reflections compute reflections based on the rendered image, while refraction mapping uses precomputed refraction patterns to distort the background image as seen through the liquid.

For gases, lighting models focus on simulating the scattering and absorption of light inside the gas volume. Techniques such as volumetric lighting and participating media models are employed to achieve this. Volumetric lighting computes the scattering of light as it passes through the gas, creating effects such as god rays and light shafts. Participating media models simulate the absorption and scattering of light by the gas particles, resulting in realistic effects such as smoke and fog.

Performance optimization is a critical consideration in real-time fluid rendering. Achieving interactive frame rates requires efficient algorithms and data structures that can handle the computational demands of fluid simulation and rendering. Techniques such as spatial partitioning and level of detail (LOD) are commonly used to optimize performance. Spatial partitioning divides the simulation domain into smaller regions, allowing for efficient computation and rendering of fluid interactions inside each region. Level of detail techniques adjust the complexity of the simulation and rendering based on the viewer's distance and perspective, reducing computational load without sacrificing visual quality.

Hardware acceleration is another key factor in achieving real-time performance. Modern graphics processing units (GPUs) are well-suited for the parallel nature of fluid simulations, enabling significant speedups. Developers leverage GPU programming frameworks such as CUDA and OpenCL to implement fluid simulation algorithms on the GPU. This allows for the efficient computation of fluid dynamics and the real-time rendering of fluid surfaces and volumes.

In addition to traditional rendering techniques, recent advancements in machine learning have opened new possibilities for real-time fluid rendering. Machine learning models can be trained to predict fluid behavior and generate realistic visual effects based on training data from high-fidelity simulations. These models can be integrated into the rendering pipeline to accelerate computations and enhance visual fidelity. For example, neural networks can be used to generate high-quality surface reconstructions or to predict the scattering and absorption properties of gases.

Interactive control and user input are essential components of real-time fluid rendering in game engines. Players expect to interact with fluids in a natural and responsive manner, whether it's splashing water, blowing smoke, or manipulating fire. To achieve this, developers implement physics-based interaction models that respond to user input and environmental changes. These models ensure that fluid simulations remain stable and visually consistent while allowing for dynamic and interactive gameplay.

In conclusion, real-time rendering of liquids and gases is a multifaceted challenge that requires the integration of physical simulation, graphical representation, and performance optimization. By employing a combination of particle systems, grid-based methods, and advanced rendering techniques, developers can create visually convincing and interactive fluid simulations in game engines. As technology continues to advance, the possibilities for real-time fluid rendering will expand, enabling even more immersive and realistic virtual environments.

Optimizing Fluid Simulations for Performance

Fluid simulations are indispensable for creating realistic and immersive environments in modern video games. However, the computational demands of simulating liquid and gas behaviors can be substantial, often challenging the limits of real-time processing capabilities. To ensure fluid simulations run efficiently without compromising visual fidelity, developers must employ a variety of optimization techniques. This section explores the strategies and methodologies that can be utilized to optimize fluid simulations, making them suitable for performance-intensive applications such as video games.

One of the primary considerations in optimizing fluid simulations is the choice of numerical methods. Different methods offer varying trade-offs between computational cost and accuracy. For instance, while some methods provide high fidelity, they may require significant processing power. Selecting the right numerical approach based on the specific needs of the simulation can lead to substantial performance gains. Simplified models and approximations can often be employed to reduce computational complexity without significantly affecting the visual outcome.

Adaptive techniques are a cornerstone of optimization in fluid simulations. These techniques dynamically adjust the level of detail based on the complexity of the fluid's behavior in different regions of the simulation domain. For example, areas with turbulent or highly dynamic fluid motion can be simulated with greater detail, while regions with relatively calm fluid behavior can be computed using coarser approximations. By concentrating computational resources where they are most needed, adaptive techniques can significantly enhance performance. Methods such as adaptive mesh refinement (AMR) and multiresolution grids are commonly used to implement this strategy.

Parallel computing is another powerful tool for optimizing fluid simulations. Modern processors, including multi-core CPUs and GPUs, are well-suited to the parallel nature of fluid dynamics computations. By distributing the workload across multiple processing units, developers can achieve substantial speedups. Parallel algorithms must be carefully designed to minimize inter-process communication and ensure load balancing among processors. Techniques such as domain decomposition, where the simulation domain is divided into smaller subdomains, are often employed to facilitate parallel processing.

Data structures play a crucial role in the efficiency of fluid simulations. Optimized data structures can reduce memory usage and improve access times, leading to faster computations. Sparse data structures, for instance, can be used to represent fluid properties only in regions where fluid is present, avoiding the overhead of storing and processing empty space. Additionally, data structures that support efficient neighbor searches, such as spatial hashing or kd-trees, can expedite the computation of interactions between fluid particles or grid cells.

Another critical aspect of optimization is the handling of boundary conditions. Accurate and efficient boundary conditions are essential for realistic fluid behavior, but they can also be computationally intensive. Techniques such as ghost cells, where additional cells are added to the simulation grid to represent boundaries, can simplify the implementation of boundary conditions and reduce computational overhead. Additionally, specialized algorithms for handling complex boundary interactions, such as fluid-solid coupling, can improve both performance and accuracy.

Temporal coherence can be exploited to enhance the efficiency of fluid simulations. Fluid behavior often exhibits temporal continuity, meaning that the state of the fluid at one time step is similar to its state at the previous time step. By leveraging this continuity, developers can reduce the computational burden of each time step. Techniques such as temporal interpolation, where fluid properties are estimated based on previous time steps, can provide accurate results with fewer computations. Additionally, adaptive time-stepping algorithms can adjust the simulation time step based on the rate of change in fluid behavior, ensuring stability and efficiency.

Optimization also extends to the rendering of fluid simulations. Efficient rendering techniques are crucial for achieving real-time performance while maintaining visual quality. For instance, level of detail (LOD) rendering can be used to adjust the complexity of the rendered fluid based on the viewer's distance and perspective. Close-up views may require high-detail rendering, while distant views can be rendered with lower detail. Additionally, techniques such as screen-space effects and shader optimizations can enhance the visual appearance of fluids without incurring high computational costs.

Machine learning has emerged as a promising tool for optimizing fluid simulations. By training neural networks on high-fidelity simulation data, developers can create surrogate models that approximate fluid behavior with significantly reduced computational demands. These models can be integrated into the simulation pipeline to provide real-time predictions of fluid dynamics. For example, a neural network might predict the overall flow pattern of a fluid, while traditional numerical methods refine the details. This hybrid approach leverages the strengths of both machine learning and conventional techniques to achieve efficient and accurate simulations.

Hardware acceleration is another key factor in optimizing fluid simulations. Graphics processing units (GPUs) are particularly well-suited for the parallel nature of fluid computations, and leveraging their capabilities can lead to significant performance improvements. Developers can use GPU programming frameworks such as CUDA or OpenCL to implement fluid simulation algorithms on the GPU. This allows for the efficient execution of computationally intensive tasks, such as particle advection and pressure solving, in parallel across thousands of GPU cores.

Profiling and performance analysis are essential steps in the optimization process. By identifying bottlenecks and hotspots in the simulation code, developers can target specific areas for optimization. Tools such as profilers and performance analyzers provide insights into the computational cost of different parts of the simulation, enabling developers to make informed decisions about where to focus their optimization efforts. Common strategies include optimizing memory access patterns, reducing redundant computations, and minimizing communication overhead in parallel algorithms.

In summary, optimizing fluid simulations for performance involves a multifaceted approach that combines numerical methods, adaptive techniques, parallel computing, and efficient data structures. By carefully selecting and implementing these strategies, developers can create fluid simulations that are both realistic and computationally feasible for real-time applications. As technology continues to advance, new opportunities for optimization will undoubtedly emerge, further enhancing the capabilities of fluid simulations in game engines.

Character Physics: Implementing Realistic Movement And Behavior

Character Animation and Physics Integration

Achieving realism in character movement inside a game environment requires a seamless blend of animation and physics. This integration is crucial for creating believable and engaging virtual worlds where characters move fluidly and respond naturally to their surroundings. In this section, we will delve into the methods and practices involved in merging character animation with physics, ensuring that each character's actions are coherent and lifelike.

To begin with, it is essential to understand the distinction between animation and physics in the context of game development. Animation typically involves pre-defined sequences of movements created by animators, often using keyframes or motion capture data. These sequences dictate how a character moves, jumps, or performs various actions. Physics, on the other hand, governs the interactions of objects inside the game world based on the laws of physics, such as gravity, friction, and collision response. The challenge lies in harmonizing these two components so that animated characters can interact with the game environment in a physically plausible manner.

One effective approach to integrating animation and physics is through the use of Inverse Kinematics (IK). IK is a technique that adjusts the position of a character's joints to achieve a desired end effector position, such as a hand or foot. By employing IK, developers can ensure that character animations adapt dynamically to the game environment. For instance, when a character walks on uneven terrain, IK can adjust the position of the feet to match the contours of the ground, resulting in a more natural gait. This method enhances the believability of character movements by allowing them to respond to environmental changes in real-time.

Another crucial aspect of this integration is the implementation of ragdoll physics. Ragdoll physics involves simulating the character's body as a collection of interconnected rigid bodies, which can react dynamically to external forces. This technique is particularly useful for simulating realistic falls, impacts, and other physical interactions. By blending ragdoll physics with traditional animations, developers can create transitions that feel smooth and authentic. For example, when a character is hit by an object, the animation can transition seamlessly to a ragdoll state, allowing the character to collapse naturally based on the impact's force and direction.

Furthermore, the incorporation of procedural animation techniques can significantly enhance the realism of character movements. Procedural animation involves generating animations algorithmically rather than relying solely on pre-defined sequences. This approach enables characters to adapt their movements to varying conditions and stimuli. For instance, a character might alter their walking speed based on the slope of the terrain or adjust their posture when carrying a heavy object. Procedural animation provides a level of flexibility and responsiveness that is difficult to achieve with traditional keyframe animations alone.

In addition to these techniques, the use of physics-based constraints can play a pivotal role in ensuring that character animations adhere to the laws of physics. Constraints are rules that restrict the movement of certain joints or body parts, ensuring that they behave in a physically plausible manner. For example, a constraint might prevent a character's arm from bending in an unnatural direction or ensure that a character's feet remain planted on the ground during a jump. By applying these constraints, developers can maintain the integrity of character movements while still allowing for dynamic interactions with the game environment.

Moreover, the integration of physics and animation can be enhanced through the use of blend trees. Blend trees are hierarchical structures that blend multiple animations based on certain parameters, such as speed, direction, or external forces. This technique allows for smooth transitions between different animations, creating a more cohesive and fluid movement. For example, a character might blend between walking, jogging, and running animations based on their speed, or transition from a standing to a crouching position based on player input. Blend trees provide a robust framework for managing complex animation states and ensuring that character movements remain coherent and responsive.

Finally, it is important to consider the role of real-time physics simulations in achieving realistic character behavior. Real-time simulations calculate the effects of physical forces on characters and objects as the game progresses, allowing for dynamic and interactive environments. By incorporating real-time physics, developers can create scenarios where characters respond naturally to various stimuli, such as wind, explosions, or collisions. This level of interactivity enhances the immersion of the game world and provides players with a more engaging and believable experience.

To sum up, the integration of character animation and physics is a multifaceted process that requires a careful balance of techniques and methodologies. By leveraging tools such as Inverse Kinematics, ragdoll physics, procedural animation, physics-based constraints, blend trees, and real-time physics simulations, developers can create characters that move and behave in a realistic and compelling manner. This integration not only enhances the visual fidelity of the game but also contributes to a more immersive and enjoyable player experience. As game development continues to evolve, the pursuit of realism in character movement will remain a critical aspect of creating engaging and lifelike virtual worlds.

Inverse Kinematics (IK) is a cornerstone technique in game development, particularly when striving for lifelike character movement. This method stands in contrast to Forward Kinematics (FK), where joint rotations are specified to achieve a particular pose. Instead, IK works by determining the necessary joint angles to place an end effector, such as a hand or foot, in a desired position. This approach is invaluable for creating dynamic and responsive character movements that adapt in real-time to the game environment.

One of the primary advantages of IK is its ability to handle complex interactions with the environment. For example, when a character reaches out to grab an object, IK can calculate the necessary adjustments to the arm's joints, ensuring that the hand aligns perfectly with the target. This capability extends beyond simple reach tasks; it can be employed to adjust a character's posture based on the terrain or to ensure that feet make proper contact with uneven surfaces. The versatility of IK makes it a powerful tool for achieving realism in character animations.

Implementing IK involves several mathematical concepts and algorithms. One widely used algorithm is the Jacobian Inverse method, which iteratively adjusts joint angles to minimize the distance between the end effector and the target position. This method is particularly effective for characters with multiple joints, such as humanoid figures, where precise control over limb movement is essential. Another common approach is the Cyclic Coordinate Descent (CCD) algorithm, which simplifies the problem by adjusting one joint at a time in a sequential manner. CCD is computationally efficient and well-suited for real-time applications, making it a popular choice in game development.

The integration of IK into a game engine requires careful consideration of performance and stability. Real-time calculations must be optimized to ensure that character movements remain fluid and responsive without causing significant computational overhead. One strategy for achieving this balance is to use a hybrid approach, combining IK with pre-defined animations. In this setup, IK is applied selectively, only when dynamic adjustments are necessary. For instance, a character might use pre-defined walking animations for general movement, while IK is employed to adjust foot placement on uneven terrain. This hybrid method allows developers to leverage the strengths of both IK and traditional animation techniques.

Another critical aspect of IK implementation is the management of joint constraints. In a real-world scenario, joints have physical limitations that prevent them from bending or rotating beyond certain angles. These constraints must be replicated in the IK system to ensure that character movements remain plausible and anatomically correct. For example, the elbow joint should not bend backwards, and the knee should only flex inside a specific range. Incorporating these constraints into the IK solver helps maintain the integrity of character animations and prevents unnatural poses.

In addition to joint constraints, developers must also consider the impact of external forces on character movement. In many game scenarios, characters interact with various dynamic elements, such as moving platforms, obstacles, or other characters. IK can be used to adjust limb positions in response to these interactions, ensuring that characters react appropriately to their surroundings. For example, when a character stands on a moving platform, IK can adjust the foot placement to maintain balance and stability. This level of interactivity enhances the realism of the game world and provides players with a more immersive experience.

The visual quality of IK-driven animations can be further enhanced through the use of blending techniques. Blending involves smoothly transitioning between different animation states to create seamless and natural movements. For instance, a character might blend between a running animation and an IK-driven reach animation when grabbing an object while in motion. By carefully managing these transitions, developers can avoid abrupt changes in posture or movement, resulting in a more polished and realistic appearance.

Another advanced application of IK is in the simulation of secondary motion. Secondary motion refers to the subtle movements that occur as a result of primary actions, such as the swaying of hair or the jiggling of clothing. IK can be used to simulate these secondary effects by adjusting joint angles in response to the primary movement. For example, when a character jumps, IK can be applied to ensure that the limbs and torso respond naturally to the forces involved, creating a more convincing portrayal of physical exertion.

Moreover, IK can be combined with other procedural animation techniques to achieve even greater levels of realism. Procedural animation involves generating animations algorithmically based on specific rules or parameters. By integrating IK with procedural methods, developers can create characters that adapt their movements to a wide range of conditions and stimuli. For instance, a character might use IK to adjust their posture when carrying a heavy object, while procedural animation determines the overall movement pattern based on the object's weight and shape. This combination allows for highly responsive and context-aware character behaviors.

In conclusion, Inverse Kinematics is a vital technique for creating realistic character movement in game development. Its ability to dynamically adjust joint angles based on target positions and environmental interactions makes it an essential tool for achieving lifelike animations. By implementing IK with careful consideration of performance, joint constraints, and external forces, developers can create characters that move and behave in a believable manner. The integration of blending techniques, secondary motion simulation, and procedural animation further enhances the visual quality and responsiveness of IK-driven animations. As game development continues to advance, the role of IK in achieving realistic character movement will remain a critical aspect of creating engaging and immersive virtual worlds.

Simulating Biomechanics in Game Characters

In game development, creating characters that move and behave in ways that mirror real-life biomechanics is a sophisticated and multifaceted challenge. The study of biomechanics involves understanding the mechanical principles of living organisms, particularly their movement and structure. Applying these principles to game characters requires a blend of anatomical knowledge, physics simulation, and computational techniques. This section explores the intricacies of simulating biomechanics in game characters, focusing on the methods and technologies that enable realistic and engaging virtual beings.

To begin with, a fundamental aspect of simulating biomechanics is accurately modeling the skeletal structure of game characters. The skeleton serves as the framework upon which all movements are based. In human and humanoid characters, this involves creating a digital representation of bones and joints that mimic the human skeletal system. Each bone must be correctly positioned and oriented, with joints allowing for realistic degrees of freedom. For instance, the elbow joint should permit flexion and extension, while the shoulder joint should enable a wider range of motion, including rotation. By meticulously replicating the human skeleton, developers lay the groundwork for lifelike character movements.

Once the skeletal structure is established, the next step is to simulate the muscular system. Muscles are responsible for generating the forces necessary for movement, and their accurate representation is crucial for realistic biomechanics. In game development, this often involves the use of muscle simulations that calculate the tension and contraction of virtual muscles. These simulations can be driven by various algorithms that model the behavior of muscles under different conditions, such as exertion and fatigue. By incorporating muscle dynamics, characters can exhibit more natural and varied movements, such as the way muscles bulge during exertion or relax when at rest.

Another critical component of biomechanical simulation is the representation of soft tissues, including skin and connective tissues. These elements contribute to the overall appearance and movement of characters. Soft tissue simulation involves modeling the deformation and elasticity of skin and other tissues in response to underlying muscle and bone movements. Techniques such as finite element analysis (FEA) can be employed to simulate the complex interactions between different layers of tissue. This results in more realistic animations, where skin stretches and compresses naturally, and characters exhibit lifelike responses to physical interactions, such as being touched or impacted by external forces.

In addition to skeletal, muscular, and soft tissue simulations, biomechanics also encompasses the modeling of joint mechanics. Joints are pivotal in determining the range and type of movements a character can perform. Each joint must be carefully modeled to allow for realistic articulation while preventing unnatural motions. This involves defining the constraints and limits of each joint, such as the maximum angle of rotation or the range of flexion. By accurately simulating joint mechanics, developers can ensure that character movements are both plausible and anatomically correct, avoiding unrealistic poses or dislocations.

One of the advanced techniques for simulating biomechanics in game characters is the use of physics-based animation. This approach leverages the laws of physics to drive character movements, rather than relying solely on pre-defined animations. By applying forces and torques to the skeletal structure, characters can move in ways that are dynamically responsive to their environment. For example, a character walking on a slippery surface might exhibit a different gait compared to walking on solid ground. Physics-based animation allows for a high degree of realism and adaptability, as characters can respond to various stimuli and conditions in real-time.

Moreover, the integration of motion capture data can significantly enhance the realism of biomechanical simulations. Motion capture involves recording the movements of real actors and translating these motions into digital characters. This technology captures the nuances of human movement, including subtle shifts in weight and balance. By incorporating motion capture data into biomechanical simulations, developers can create characters that move with a level of authenticity that is difficult to achieve through traditional keyframe animation alone. Additionally, motion capture can be combined with physics-based approaches to further refine character behavior, ensuring that movements are both realistic and contextually appropriate.

Another important aspect of simulating biomechanics is the consideration of character interactions with their environment. Characters must be able to navigate and respond to various terrains, obstacles, and other dynamic elements inside the game world. This involves simulating the interactions between the character's body and the environment, such as the way feet make contact with the ground or how hands grasp objects. Techniques such as collision detection and response are essential for ensuring that characters interact with their surroundings in a believable manner. By accurately modeling these interactions, developers can create immersive and engaging experiences where characters move and behave in ways that are consistent with the physical properties of the game world.

Furthermore, the use of procedural animation techniques can enhance the realism of biomechanical simulations. Procedural animation involves generating animations algorithmically based on specific rules or parameters. This allows characters to adapt their movements to a wide range of conditions and stimuli. For instance, a character might adjust their posture when carrying a heavy load or change their gait when walking on uneven terrain. Procedural animation provides a level of flexibility and responsiveness that is difficult to achieve with traditional animation methods alone. By combining procedural techniques with biomechanical simulations, developers can create characters that exhibit highly dynamic and context-aware behaviors.

In conclusion, simulating biomechanics in game characters is a complex but rewarding endeavor that involves a deep understanding of anatomy, physics, and computational techniques. By accurately modeling skeletal structures, muscle dynamics, soft tissues, joint mechanics, and environmental interactions, developers can create characters that move and behave in ways that are strikingly realistic. The integration of motion capture data and procedural animation further enhances the authenticity and adaptability of character movements. As game development continues to advance, the simulation of biomechanics will remain a critical aspect of creating lifelike and engaging virtual beings, offering players immersive experiences that closely mirror the intricacies of real-world movement and behavior.

Dynamic Interaction with the Game Environment

Dynamic interaction with the game environment is a fundamental aspect of creating an immersive and believable gaming experience. This section delves into the techniques and principles that enable characters to interact dynamically with their surroundings, ensuring that their movements and behaviors are coherent and lifelike.

When designing character interactions, one of the primary considerations is the environment's physical properties. These properties include elements such as surface textures, material densities, and environmental forces like wind or water currents. By accurately simulating these properties, developers can create a world where characters respond naturally to their surroundings. For instance, a character walking on a muddy surface should leave footprints and experience resistance, while the same character on a polished floor might slide or lose traction.

To achieve this level of detail, developers often employ a combination of collision detection algorithms and physics simulations. Collision detection ensures that characters and objects inside the game world interact correctly, preventing them from passing through one another. This involves calculating the points of contact and the resulting forces that should be applied. For example, when a character bumps into a wall, the collision detection system identifies the point of impact and generates a response force that pushes the character back. This interaction must be handled with precision to avoid unnatural or jarring movements.

The physics simulation then takes over, applying the laws of physics to dictate how characters and objects should behave upon collision. This includes calculating the effects of gravity, friction, and elasticity. Gravity ensures that characters remain grounded unless acted upon by another force, while friction determines how easily they can move across different surfaces. Elasticity, on the other hand, governs how objects bounce or deform upon impact. By fine-tuning these parameters, developers can create realistic interactions that enhance the overall immersion of the game.

Another critical aspect of dynamic interaction is the use of environmental triggers and events. These are predefined conditions inside the game world that cause specific reactions when characters interact with them. For example, stepping on a pressure plate might open a hidden door, or walking through a patch of tall grass could trigger the appearance of hidden creatures. These triggers add an element of unpredictability and engagement, encouraging players to explore and interact with their surroundings.

To implement environmental triggers effectively, developers must define the conditions under which they are activated and the resulting actions. This often involves scripting languages or visual scripting tools that allow for the creation of complex behaviors without extensive coding. For instance, a script might define that when a character's position intersects with a specific trigger zone, a series of events is set into motion. These events could range from simple animations to complex sequences involving multiple characters and objects.

In addition to predefined triggers, real-time environmental changes play a significant role in dynamic interaction. These changes can be driven by player actions or occur independently as part of the game's narrative. For example, a character might cause a bridge to collapse by walking on it, or a sudden storm could alter the landscape, creating new obstacles and challenges. Real-time changes require the game engine to continuously update the state of the environment and adjust character behaviors accordingly.

One effective technique for managing real-time changes is the use of event-driven programming. This paradigm allows for the decoupling of game logic, making it easier to handle multiple events simultaneously. In an event-driven system, characters and objects subscribe to specific events and react when those events are triggered. For example, a character might subscribe to an "earthquake" event and execute a specific animation sequence when the event occurs. This approach enables a more modular and scalable design, allowing developers to create complex interactions without overwhelming the system.

Furthermore, the integration of artificial intelligence (AI) can significantly enhance dynamic interaction by enabling characters to make decisions based on environmental cues. AI systems can analyze the state of the game world and determine the most appropriate actions for characters to take. For instance, an AI-controlled character might seek shelter during a rainstorm or avoid hazardous areas based on terrain analysis. By incorporating AI, developers can create more adaptive and responsive characters that enhance the realism of the game.

One of the challenges in implementing AI-driven interactions is ensuring that the decision-making process is both efficient and believable. This often involves balancing the complexity of AI algorithms with the need for real-time performance. Techniques such as behavior trees and finite state machines are commonly used to manage AI behaviors, providing a structured framework for decision-making. These techniques allow developers to define a hierarchy of actions and conditions, enabling characters to respond appropriately to a wide range of scenarios.

In addition to AI, procedural generation can be employed to create dynamic and varied environments that enhance interaction. Procedural generation involves using algorithms to generate content on-the-fly, rather than relying on pre-designed assets. This approach can create unique and unpredictable environments, encouraging players to adapt their strategies and interactions. For example, a procedurally generated dungeon might offer different layouts, traps, and enemies each time it is explored, providing a fresh experience with every playthrough.

To implement procedural generation effectively, developers must define the rules and parameters that govern the generation process. This includes specifying the types of elements that can be generated, their distribution, and the relationships between them. For instance, a procedural terrain generator might use noise functions to create realistic landscapes, while a dungeon generator might use graph-based algorithms to create interconnected rooms and corridors. By carefully designing these rules, developers can create dynamic environments that feel both natural and challenging.

Another important consideration in dynamic interaction is the feedback provided to players. Effective feedback ensures that players understand the consequences of their actions and can make informed decisions. This feedback can be visual, auditory, or haptic, providing multiple channels of information. For example, visual cues such as dust clouds or debris can indicate the impact of a character's actions, while sound effects can enhance the sense of immersion. Haptic feedback, such as controller vibrations, can provide tactile sensations that reinforce the physicality of interactions.

To finalize, dynamic interaction with the game environment is a multifaceted process that requires careful consideration of physical properties, collision detection, environmental triggers, real-time changes, AI, procedural generation, and player feedback. By leveraging these techniques, developers can create immersive and engaging game worlds where characters interact naturally with their surroundings. This not only enhances the realism of the game but also provides players with a richer and more satisfying experience. As game development continues to evolve, the pursuit of dynamic interaction will remain a critical aspect of creating believable and captivating virtual environments.

Procedural Generation of Character Behaviors

Procedural generation is a powerful technique in game development that allows for the creation of diverse and dynamic content using algorithms and rulesets. When applied to character behaviors, procedural generation can produce a wide variety of actions and reactions that make characters appear more lifelike and responsive to their environment. This section explores the principles and methods behind procedural generation of character behaviors, highlighting its benefits, challenges, and practical implementation strategies.

One of the primary advantages of procedural generation is its ability to create unique and unpredictable behaviors without the need for extensive manual scripting. By defining a set of rules and parameters, developers can generate a vast array of possible actions that characters can perform. This not only saves time but also enhances the replayability of a game, as players encounter different behaviors in each playthrough. For instance, in a survival game, procedural generation can determine how non-player characters (NPCs) search for resources, build shelters, or interact with each other, resulting in a dynamic and engaging experience.

To implement procedural generation of character behaviors, developers must first establish a robust framework that can handle the complexity and variability of generated actions. This involves defining a behavior model that outlines the possible states and transitions a character can undergo. A common approach is to use finite state machines (FSMs) or behavior trees, which provide a structured way to manage different states and the conditions that trigger transitions between them. For example, an FSM for a guard character might include states such as "patrol," "alert," and "chase," with transitions based on factors like player proximity and line of sight.

Once the behavior model is in place, developers can introduce randomness and variability through procedural algorithms. These algorithms can be designed to generate different behaviors based on predefined probabilities, environmental factors, or character attributes. For instance, a procedural algorithm might determine that a character has a 30% chance of choosing to hide when threatened, a 50% chance of fleeing, and a 20% chance of fighting back. By adjusting these probabilities and incorporating additional variables, developers can create a wide range of behaviors that make characters feel more dynamic and less predictable.

Another key aspect of procedural generation is the use of environmental cues to influence character behaviors. Characters can be programmed to respond to various stimuli in their surroundings, such as changes in lighting, sounds, or the presence of other characters. For example, a procedurally generated behavior might involve an NPC seeking shelter when it starts to rain, or becoming more cautious when entering a dark area. By incorporating environmental cues, developers can create characters that appear more aware and adaptive, enhancing the overall immersion of the game world.

In addition to environmental cues, procedural generation can also take into account character-specific attributes and traits. These attributes can include factors such as health, stamina, morale, and personality, which influence how a character behaves in different situations. For instance, a character with high stamina might be more likely to engage in physically demanding actions, while a character with low morale might be prone to fleeing or surrendering. By integrating these attributes into the procedural algorithms, developers can create more nuanced and individualized behaviors that reflect the unique characteristics of each character.

One of the challenges of procedural generation is ensuring that the generated behaviors remain coherent and believable. While randomness and variability are essential for creating dynamic behaviors, they must be balanced with logical consistency to avoid jarring or nonsensical actions. To achieve this balance, developers can use a combination of rule-based systems and machine learning techniques. Rule-based systems provide a set of guidelines that constrain the possible behaviors, ensuring they align with the game's logic and narrative. Machine learning, on the other hand, can be used to refine and optimize the behavior generation process based on data and feedback, resulting in more realistic and polished behaviors over time.

Moreover, procedural generation can be enhanced by incorporating social dynamics and interactions between characters. Characters can be programmed to form relationships, alliances, or rivalries based on their interactions and experiences. For example, procedural algorithms can determine that characters who frequently cooperate on tasks develop a bond, while those who compete for resources become adversaries. These social dynamics can add an additional layer of depth and complexity to character behaviors, making the game world feel more alive and interconnected.

Another practical implementation strategy for procedural generation is the use of modular behavior components. By breaking down behaviors into smaller, reusable modules, developers can create a library of actions that can be combined in various ways to produce diverse behaviors. For instance, a modular approach might involve creating separate components for movement, combat, and interaction, which can be dynamically assembled based on the character's current state and context. This modularity allows for greater flexibility and scalability, as new behaviors can be easily added or modified without overhauling the entire system.

Furthermore, procedural generation can be complemented by player-driven input and customization. Allowing players to influence or modify character behaviors through gameplay choices or customization options can enhance the sense of agency and personalization. For example, players might be able to train or equip their characters with specific skills that affect their procedural behaviors, or make decisions that shape the character's personality and tendencies. By integrating player input, developers can create a more interactive and engaging experience that resonates with individual playstyles and preferences.

To sum it all up, procedural generation of character behaviors is a powerful tool for creating dynamic, diverse, and lifelike actions in game development. By leveraging algorithms, environmental cues, character attributes, and social dynamics, developers can produce a wide range of behaviors that enhance the realism and immersion of the game world. While challenges such as maintaining coherence and balance exist, practical strategies such as rule-based systems, machine learning, modular components, and player-driven customization can help overcome these obstacles. As game development continues to evolve, procedural generation will remain a vital technique for crafting engaging and believable character behaviors, offering players rich and varied experiences in virtual environments.

Handling Character State Transitions Smoothly

In the intricate world of game design, the fluidity with which characters transition between different states is paramount to creating an immersive and believable experience. These state transitions, encompassing actions such as running, jumping, or even subtle shifts in posture, must be handled with precision to maintain the illusion of life and responsiveness. This section delves into the principles and techniques essential for achieving smooth character state transitions, ensuring that every movement appears natural and seamless.

One of the foundational aspects of managing state transitions is the development of a comprehensive state machine. A state machine is a conceptual model that defines the various states a character can inhabit and the conditions under which transitions occur. This framework is crucial for organizing and controlling the multitude of actions a character can perform. For example, a character might have states such as idle, walking, sprinting, and crouching. Each state is defined by specific animations and behaviors, and the transitions between these states are governed by predefined rules. By meticulously designing this state machine, developers can create a robust system that supports fluid transitions.

The transition rules inside the state machine are critical for ensuring smooth state changes. These rules typically involve conditions based on player input, environmental factors, or internal character attributes. For instance, a character might transition from walking to running when the player holds down a sprint button, or shift from idle to crouching when approaching a low obstacle. The key to smooth transitions lies in the careful definition of these conditions and the implementation of blending techniques that interpolate between animations. Blending allows for a gradual and natural shift from one animation to another, avoiding abrupt or jarring changes that can break immersion.

Animation blending plays a pivotal role in achieving seamless state transitions. Blending involves the interpolation of two or more animations to create a smooth transition. This technique can be executed using linear interpolation (LERP) or more advanced methods such as cubic interpolation, which provides a smoother curve. For example, when a character transitions from walking to running, blending ensures that the movement accelerates gradually, with the animations merging fluidly. The duration and weight of the blend can be adjusted to match the desired level of smoothness, with longer blends resulting in more gradual transitions.

In addition to blending, developers must consider the timing and synchronization of animations. Timing refers to the precise moment at which a transition occurs, while synchronization ensures that different parts of the character's body move in harmony during the transition. For instance, when a character stops running and begins to crouch, the timing of the transition should coincide with the character's footfalls to maintain a realistic gait. Synchronization ensures that the character's upper body and lower body move cohesively, preventing disjointed or unnatural movements. By fine-tuning timing and synchronization, developers can enhance the realism and fluidity of state transitions.

Another critical aspect of handling state transitions is the use of inverse kinematics (IK). IK is a computational technique that adjusts the positions of a character's joints to achieve a desired end effector position, such as placing a hand on a surface or aligning feet with uneven terrain. By incorporating IK into state transitions, developers can ensure that the character's limbs move naturally and interact appropriately with the environment. For example, when transitioning from standing to crouching, IK can adjust the character's legs to maintain contact with the ground, enhancing the realism of the movement.

The integration of physics-based systems can also contribute to smoother state transitions. Physics-based systems simulate the forces and constraints acting on a character, allowing for more dynamic and responsive movements. For instance, a character transitioning from running to jumping can benefit from physics simulations that account for momentum and gravity, resulting in a more realistic leap. By combining physics-based systems with traditional animation techniques, developers can achieve a higher degree of realism and fluidity in state transitions.

Furthermore, the use of procedural animation techniques can enhance the flexibility and adaptability of state transitions. Procedural animation involves generating animations algorithmically based on specific rules or parameters. This approach allows characters to adapt their movements to a wide range of conditions and stimuli. For example, a procedural animation system might adjust a character's gait based on the incline of the terrain or the weight of an object being carried. By incorporating procedural techniques, developers can create characters that exhibit highly dynamic and context-aware behaviors, resulting in smoother and more natural state transitions.

In addition to technical considerations, the narrative and contextual aspects of state transitions should not be overlooked. The context in which a transition occurs can significantly impact its perceived smoothness and believability. For example, a character transitioning from a calm walk to a frantic sprint should convey a sense of urgency and purpose. This can be achieved through the use of contextual animations, sound effects, and visual cues that reinforce the narrative. By aligning state transitions with the story and context, developers can enhance the overall immersion and emotional impact of the game.

Testing and iteration are essential components of refining state transitions. The complexity of character movements and the multitude of possible transitions necessitate thorough testing to identify and address any issues. Playtesting with a diverse group of players can provide valuable feedback on the smoothness and responsiveness of state transitions. Iterative refinement, based on player feedback and performance metrics, allows developers to fine-tune the system and achieve the desired level of fluidity and realism.

To summarize, handling character state transitions smoothly is a multifaceted challenge that requires a blend of technical expertise, creative design, and iterative refinement. By developing a comprehensive state machine, implementing blending techniques, fine-tuning timing and synchronization, incorporating inverse kinematics and physics-based systems, leveraging procedural animation, and considering narrative context, developers can create characters that move and behave in ways that are natural and believable. The pursuit of smooth state transitions is essential for creating immersive and engaging game experiences, where every movement contributes to the illusion of life and responsiveness. As game development continues to advance, the techniques and principles discussed in this section will remain critical for achieving the highest levels of realism and fluidity in character animations.

Physics-Based Character Controllers and AI

In the realm of game development, the creation of lifelike characters hinges on the effective implementation of physics-based character controllers and artificial intelligence (AI). These two components work in tandem to ensure that characters not only move in a believable manner but also exhibit behaviors that respond dynamically to the game world. This section delves into the intricacies of designing and integrating physics-based character controllers, alongside the role of AI in enhancing character realism and interactivity.

To begin with, the foundation of any physics-based character controller lies in its ability to simulate realistic physical interactions. This involves the application of physical laws such as inertia, momentum, and force to govern character movement. Unlike traditional animation-driven controllers, physics-based controllers allow for more natural and responsive interactions with the environment. For instance, when a character accelerates, the controller must account for the gradual increase in speed, ensuring that the movement appears fluid and realistic. Similarly, when coming to a stop, the character should decelerate in a manner consistent with physical principles.

One of the critical aspects of designing a physics-based character controller is the accurate simulation of body mechanics. This includes the implementation of a skeletal structure that mimics human or creature anatomy, complete with joints and muscles. By simulating the forces acting on these joints, developers can achieve a high degree of realism in character movement. For example, when a character jumps, the controller must simulate the force exerted by the legs and the resulting trajectory of the body. This requires precise calculations to ensure that the jump height, distance, and landing are all physically plausible.

In addition to body mechanics, the interaction between characters and the environment plays a pivotal role in realism. A physics-based character controller must account for various environmental factors such as terrain, obstacles, and surfaces. For instance, when a character walks on a slope, the controller must adjust the character's posture and movement to reflect the incline. This involves calculating the impact of gravity and friction on the character's motion. Similarly, when navigating obstacles, the controller must ensure that the character's movements are adapted to the shape and size of the obstacles, allowing for smooth traversal.

Another essential component of physics-based character controllers is the management of collisions. Collisions between characters and objects are a common occurrence in games, and handling them accurately is crucial for maintaining realism. The controller must detect collisions and respond appropriately, whether it involves bouncing off surfaces, being pushed back, or coming to a halt. This requires the implementation of collision detection algorithms that can identify points of contact and calculate the resulting forces. By simulating the physical response to collisions, developers can create characters that interact convincingly with the game world.

While physics-based character controllers lay the groundwork for realistic movement, the integration of AI is what brings characters to life. AI enables characters to make decisions, exhibit behaviors, and adapt to changing situations. This is achieved through the implementation of decision-making algorithms, behavior models, and learning techniques.

One of the primary functions of AI in character controllers is pathfinding. Pathfinding algorithms allow characters to navigate the game world efficiently, avoiding obstacles and reaching their destinations. Techniques such as A* (A-star) and Dijkstra's algorithm are commonly used to calculate optimal paths. The AI must consider various factors such as terrain type, character abilities, and potential hazards when determining the best route. By incorporating pathfinding into the character controller, developers can ensure that characters move intelligently and purposefully.

In addition to pathfinding, AI plays a crucial role in decision-making and behavior. Characters must be able to assess their surroundings, evaluate potential actions, and select the most appropriate response. This involves the use of behavior trees, finite state machines, or utility-based systems to model decision-making processes. For instance, a character might need to decide whether to engage in combat, seek cover, or flee based on the current situation. The AI must weigh factors such as health, enemy strength, and available resources to make an informed decision.

Furthermore, AI can enhance character realism through the implementation of learning algorithms. These algorithms enable characters to adapt their behaviors based on experience and feedback. For example, a character might learn to avoid certain areas after encountering dangers or to use specific tactics that have proven effective in the past. Machine learning techniques such as reinforcement learning can be employed to train characters, allowing them to improve over time. By incorporating learning algorithms, developers can create characters that evolve and exhibit more complex behaviors.

The interaction between physics-based character controllers and AI extends beyond individual characters to encompass group dynamics and social interactions. AI can be used to model group behaviors, allowing characters to coordinate their actions and work together towards common goals. For instance, in a squad-based game, AI-controlled characters might communicate and strategize to flank enemies or provide cover fire. This requires the implementation of communication protocols and shared decision-making processes. By simulating group dynamics, developers can create more immersive and engaging gameplay experiences.

Moreover, AI can facilitate the customization and personalization of characters. Through the use of procedural generation techniques, AI can create unique character attributes, appearances, and behaviors. This allows for a diverse range of characters, each with distinct personalities and abilities. Players can interact with characters that feel unique and tailored to their preferences, enhancing the overall immersion and replayability of the game.

Finally, the integration of physics-based character controllers and AI requires careful consideration of performance and optimization. Real-time physics simulations and AI computations can be resource-intensive, necessitating efficient algorithms and data structures. Developers must strike a balance between realism and performance, ensuring that the game runs smoothly without compromising on the quality of character interactions. Techniques such as level-of-detail (LOD) and parallel processing can be employed to optimize performance, allowing for complex simulations without overburdening the system.

To sum up, the implementation of physics-based character controllers and AI is a multifaceted endeavor that demands a deep understanding of both physical principles and artificial intelligence. By combining these two elements, developers can create characters that move and behave in ways that are both realistic and dynamic. The interplay between physics simulations and AI-driven behaviors results in characters that respond intelligently to their environment, adapt to changing situations, and interact seamlessly with the game world. As the field of game development continues to evolve, the integration of physics-based character controllers and AI will remain a cornerstone of creating immersive and believable virtual experiences.

Optimization Techniques: Enhancing Performance In Physics Simulations

Profiling and Benchmarking Physics Simulations

In game development, the efficiency and performance of physics simulations are paramount for delivering a seamless and immersive player experience. Profiling and benchmarking are critical practices that enable developers to identify performance bottlenecks and optimize their physics engines effectively. This section delves into the methodologies and tools essential for profiling and benchmarking physics simulations, providing a comprehensive guide to enhancing performance.

Profiling Physics Simulations

Profiling is the process of collecting detailed information about the performance characteristics of a physics simulation. This involves measuring various aspects such as computation time, memory usage, and the frequency of function calls. By analyzing these metrics, developers can pinpoint inefficient areas inside the simulation code and make informed decisions about optimization.

One fundamental approach to profiling is the use of built-in profiling tools provided by game development environments. These tools offer real-time insights into the performance of physics simulations. For instance, Unity's Profiler and Unreal Engine's Profiler are powerful utilities that allow developers to monitor CPU and GPU usage, memory allocation, and execution time of physics-related tasks. By leveraging these tools, developers can visualize performance data and identify areas that require optimization.

Another essential aspect of profiling is the identification of hotspots. Hotspots are sections of code that consume a significant portion of the simulation's computational resources. These can include collision detection algorithms, physics integration steps, or constraint solvers. By isolating and analyzing these hotspots, developers can focus their optimization efforts on the most impactful areas. Techniques such as sampling profilers and instrumentation profilers can be employed to gather detailed information about function execution times and call frequencies, aiding in the identification of these critical sections.

Benchmarking Physics Simulations

Benchmarking, on the other hand, involves comparing the performance of a physics simulation against a set of predefined metrics or standards. This process helps developers understand how their simulation performs under various conditions and workloads, providing a baseline for optimization efforts.

To conduct effective benchmarking, it is crucial to establish a set of representative test cases that reflect different aspects of the physics simulation. These test cases should cover a range of scenarios, from simple interactions between a few objects to complex scenes with numerous entities and constraints. By running these test cases and measuring performance metrics such as frame rate, simulation step time, and memory consumption, developers can gain a comprehensive understanding of the simulation's performance characteristics.

Automated benchmarking frameworks can significantly streamline the benchmarking process. These frameworks allow developers to run a series of test cases in a controlled environment and collect performance data systematically. Tools like Google Benchmark and Unity Test Framework provide robust solutions for automating benchmark tests, enabling developers to track performance changes over time and evaluate the impact of optimization efforts.

Interpreting Profiling and Benchmarking Data

Once profiling and benchmarking data has been collected, the next step is to interpret the results and derive actionable insights. This involves analyzing the data to identify patterns, trends, and anomalies that indicate performance issues.

One common approach is to visualize the profiling data using graphs and charts. Visualization tools can help developers understand the distribution of computational resources across different components of the physics simulation. For example, flame graphs can be used to represent the hierarchical structure of function calls and their respective execution times, making it easier to identify bottlenecks.

Another important aspect of interpreting profiling data is the comparison of different simulation versions. By comparing the performance metrics of various iterations of the physics engine, developers can assess the effectiveness of optimization techniques and identify regressions. This iterative process ensures continuous improvement and refinement of the simulation's performance.

Optimization Strategies Based on Profiling and Benchmarking

Profiling and benchmarking provide the foundation for targeted optimization efforts. Once performance bottlenecks have been identified, developers can employ a range of optimization strategies to enhance the efficiency of physics simulations.

One effective strategy is algorithmic optimization. This involves refining the algorithms used in the simulation to reduce computational complexity and improve performance. For instance, optimizing collision detection algorithms by implementing spatial partitioning techniques such as bounding volume hierarchies or spatial hashing can significantly reduce the number of collision checks required, leading to faster simulations.

Another strategy is parallelization. By distributing the computational workload across multiple threads or processing units, developers can leverage modern hardware architectures to achieve substantial performance gains. Techniques such as task-based parallelism and data parallelism can be applied to physics simulations to maximize the utilization of available resources.

Memory management is also a critical aspect of optimization. Efficient memory allocation and deallocation can reduce overhead and improve the overall performance of the simulation. Techniques such as object pooling and memory pooling can help minimize memory fragmentation and reduce the frequency of memory allocation operations.

To summarize, profiling and benchmarking are indispensable practices for optimizing physics simulations in game engines. By systematically collecting and analyzing performance data, developers can identify bottlenecks, implement targeted optimizations, and achieve significant performance improvements. The methodologies and tools discussed in this section provide a comprehensive framework for enhancing the efficiency of physics simulations, ultimately contributing to a more immersive and responsive gaming experience.

Optimizing Memory Usage in Physics Engines

In the intricate world of game development, the efficiency of memory usage inside physics engines holds paramount importance. Effective memory management not only contributes to the performance and responsiveness of a game but also ensures that the game runs smoothly across various hardware configurations. This section delves into diverse strategies aimed at optimizing memory usage in physics engines, providing practical insights and techniques for developers seeking to enhance their simulations.

One of the foundational principles in optimizing memory usage is understanding the memory footprint of different components inside the physics engine. A physics engine typically comprises various subsystems, such as collision detection, rigid body dynamics, and constraint solvers. Each of these subsystems has distinct memory requirements and usage patterns. By profiling the memory consumption of these subsystems, developers can identify areas where memory optimization can have the most significant impact.

A key strategy in optimizing memory usage is the implementation of efficient data structures. The choice of data structures can greatly influence both the memory footprint and the performance of the physics engine. For instance, using spatial partitioning techniques, such as grids or trees, can help manage the spatial relationships between objects more efficiently. These structures reduce the amount of memory required to store spatial information and can also speed up collision detection processes.

Another effective approach is the use of memory pooling. Memory pooling involves pre-allocating a pool of memory that can be reused for objects that are frequently created and destroyed. This technique can significantly reduce the overhead associated with dynamic memory allocation and deallocation, which can be particularly beneficial in scenarios where a large number of objects are continuously interacting. By reusing memory from a pre-allocated pool, developers can minimize fragmentation and improve the overall performance of the physics engine.

In addition to memory pooling, object pooling is another technique that can be employed to optimize memory usage. Object pooling focuses on reusing instances of objects instead of creating new ones. For example, in a physics simulation where particles are frequently created and destroyed, maintaining a pool of reusable particle objects can reduce the memory overhead and improve performance. When a particle is no longer needed, it can be returned to the pool instead of being destroyed, and a new particle can be retrieved from the pool when needed. This approach not only optimizes memory usage but also reduces the time spent on object creation and destruction.

Efficient memory management also involves minimizing memory fragmentation. Fragmentation occurs when memory is allocated and deallocated in a way that leaves small, unusable gaps between memory blocks. Over time, fragmentation can lead to inefficient memory usage and reduced performance. One way to combat fragmentation is to use contiguous memory allocation for objects that are frequently accessed together. By allocating related objects in contiguous memory blocks, developers can reduce fragmentation and improve cache coherence, leading to better performance.

Another important aspect of memory optimization is the management of temporary and transient data. In a physics simulation, temporary data structures, such as intermediate calculation results or temporary buffers, are often used. Efficiently managing these temporary data structures can help reduce memory overhead. One approach is to use stack-based allocation for temporary data. Stack-based allocation involves allocating memory for temporary data on the stack, which is automatically deallocated when the function scope ends. This approach is efficient and reduces the overhead associated with dynamic memory allocation.

Developers can also leverage memory profiling tools to gain insights into memory usage patterns and identify potential areas for optimization. Memory profiling tools provide detailed information about memory allocation, usage, and deallocation, allowing developers to pinpoint memory leaks, fragmentation issues, and other inefficiencies. By analyzing the memory profiling data, developers can make informed decisions about memory optimization strategies and track the effectiveness of their optimizations over time.

To sum it all up, optimizing memory usage in physics engines is a multifaceted task that involves a combination of efficient data structures, memory pooling, object pooling, fragmentation reduction, and effective management of temporary data. By implementing these strategies, developers can enhance the performance and responsiveness of their physics simulations, ultimately contributing to a more immersive and enjoyable gaming experience. The techniques discussed in this section provide a comprehensive framework for optimizing memory usage, ensuring that physics engines run efficiently across a wide range of hardware configurations.

Parallel Processing and Multithreading Techniques

In the constantly evolving landscape of game development, the demand for realistic and responsive physics simulations has never been higher. As game worlds become more intricate and detailed, the computational burden on physics engines increases, necessitating advanced optimization strategies. One such strategy is the utilization of parallel processing and multithreading techniques, which can significantly enhance the performance of physics simulations.

Parallel processing involves dividing a computational task into smaller subtasks that can be executed simultaneously across multiple processing units. This approach leverages the capabilities of modern multi-core processors to perform numerous operations concurrently, thereby reducing the overall computation time. In the context of physics simulations, parallel processing can be applied to various components such as collision detection, rigid body dynamics, and constraint resolution.

Multithreading, a subset of parallel processing, entails the concurrent execution of multiple threads inside a single process. Each thread operates independently but shares the same memory space, enabling efficient communication and data sharing. By distributing the workload across multiple threads, developers can achieve significant performance gains, especially in physics-heavy simulations.

One of the primary challenges in implementing parallel processing and multithreading in physics simulations is ensuring thread safety. Thread safety refers to the correct and predictable behavior of a program when multiple threads access shared resources concurrently. Without proper synchronization mechanisms, race conditions can occur, leading to inconsistent and erroneous results. To mitigate this risk, developers can employ synchronization primitives such as mutexes, semaphores, and condition variables. These constructs help coordinate the execution of threads, ensuring that shared resources are accessed in a controlled manner.

Another critical aspect of parallel processing in physics simulations is the division of tasks into smaller, manageable units. This process, known as task decomposition, involves breaking down a complex simulation into independent tasks that can be executed concurrently. For example, in a particle-based simulation, each particle's motion and interactions can be computed independently, making it an ideal candidate for parallelization. By decomposing the simulation into smaller tasks, developers can distribute the workload evenly across multiple processing units, maximizing resource utilization and minimizing idle time.

Load balancing is another crucial factor in the effective implementation of parallel processing. Load balancing refers to the distribution of computational tasks across processing units to ensure that each unit is utilized optimally. In an unbalanced system, some processing units may be overloaded while others remain underutilized, leading to inefficiencies and reduced performance. Dynamic load balancing techniques, such as work stealing and task migration, can help address this issue by redistributing tasks among processing units based on their current workload. These techniques ensure that the computational load is evenly distributed, resulting in improved performance and reduced computation time.

One practical application of parallel processing in physics simulations is the use of spatial partitioning techniques. Spatial partitioning involves dividing the simulation space into smaller regions, each of which can be processed independently. Techniques such as grid-based partitioning, octrees, and k-d trees can be employed to organize the simulation space efficiently. By processing each region concurrently, developers can significantly reduce the time required for collision detection and other spatial queries, leading to faster and more responsive simulations.

In addition to spatial partitioning, developers can also leverage data parallelism to enhance the performance of physics simulations. Data parallelism involves performing the same operation on multiple data elements simultaneously. For example, in a fluid simulation, the computation of fluid properties such as pressure and velocity can be parallelized across different fluid cells. By applying the same computation to multiple data elements concurrently, developers can achieve substantial performance improvements.

Another technique that can be employed to optimize physics simulations is task-based parallelism. Task-based parallelism involves dividing the simulation into independent tasks that can be executed concurrently. Unlike data parallelism, which focuses on parallelizing operations on data elements, task-based parallelism emphasizes the concurrent execution of different tasks. For example, in a physics simulation, tasks such as collision detection, force computation, and constraint resolution can be executed in parallel. By identifying and parallelizing independent tasks, developers can achieve significant performance gains.

When implementing multithreading, it is essential to consider the overhead associated with thread management. Creating and managing threads incurs overhead, which can negate the performance benefits of parallelization if not managed correctly. Thread pools provide an effective solution to this problem by reusing a fixed number of threads for executing multiple tasks. By maintaining a pool of threads, developers can minimize the overhead associated with thread creation and destruction, resulting in more efficient multithreading.

Another consideration when implementing parallel processing and multithreading in physics simulations is the granularity of tasks. Granularity refers to the size and complexity of the tasks being parallelized. Fine-grained tasks, which are small and numerous, can lead to high overhead due to frequent synchronization and communication between threads. On the other hand, coarse-grained tasks, which are larger and fewer, may result in uneven load distribution and underutilization of processing units. Striking the right balance between fine-grained and coarse-grained tasks is crucial for achieving optimal performance in parallel processing.

The choice of parallel processing and multithreading techniques also depends on the specific requirements of the physics simulation. For real-time simulations, such as those used in interactive games, low-latency and responsiveness are critical. In such cases, techniques that minimize synchronization overhead and ensure timely task execution are preferred. For offline simulations, such as those used in scientific research or animation, throughput and accuracy may be prioritized over latency. In these scenarios, techniques that maximize resource utilization and ensure accurate results are more suitable.

To sum it all up, parallel processing and multithreading techniques offer powerful tools for enhancing the performance of physics simulations in game engines. By dividing computational tasks into smaller, manageable units and distributing them across multiple processing units, developers can achieve significant performance gains. However, implementing these techniques requires careful consideration of thread safety, task decomposition, load balancing, and overhead management. By addressing these challenges and leveraging the capabilities of modern multi-core processors, developers can create highly efficient and responsive physics simulations that meet the demands of today's complex and dynamic game worlds.

Adaptive Time Stepping for Performance Enhancement

In the domain of game physics, the accurate and efficient simulation of physical phenomena plays a crucial role in delivering an engaging and realistic player experience. One of the key aspects that influences the performance of physics simulations is the choice of time-stepping methods. Adaptive time stepping, in particular, offers a sophisticated approach to dynamically adjust the time step size based on the simulation's current state, thereby optimizing performance without sacrificing accuracy. This section delves into the principles, advantages, and implementation strategies of adaptive time stepping in the context of game physics, providing developers with practical insights to enhance their simulations.

At the core of adaptive time stepping lies the concept of dynamically varying the time step size during the simulation. Traditional fixed time-stepping methods employ a constant time step size, which can either be too large, leading to instability and inaccuracies, or too small, resulting in excessive computational overhead. Adaptive time stepping, on the other hand, adjusts the time step size in response to the simulation's evolving conditions, allowing for a more efficient allocation of computational resources.

One of the primary benefits of adaptive time stepping is its ability to maintain a delicate balance between accuracy and performance. In regions of the simulation where physical interactions are intense and rapidly changing, such as during collisions or high-speed movements, the time step size can be reduced to ensure precise calculations. Conversely, in regions where changes are gradual and less dynamic, the time step size can be increased, reducing the computational burden and enhancing overall performance. This adaptability allows developers to achieve high fidelity simulations without incurring unnecessary computational costs.

To effectively implement adaptive time stepping, it is essential to establish criteria for adjusting the time step size. One common approach is to monitor the simulation's error estimates. Error estimates provide a measure of the deviation between the simulated results and the true physical behavior. By setting predefined error thresholds, the simulation can adjust the time step size to maintain the error inside acceptable limits. For instance, if the error exceeds the upper threshold, the time step size is reduced to improve accuracy. Conversely, if the error falls below the lower threshold, the time step size is increased to enhance performance. This feedback loop ensures that the simulation remains both accurate and efficient.

Another important consideration in adaptive time stepping is the selection of integration methods. Integration methods, such as explicit, implicit, and semi-implicit methods, play a crucial role in determining the stability and accuracy of the simulation. Explicit methods, while computationally efficient, may require smaller time steps to maintain stability. Implicit methods, on the other hand, offer greater stability but at the cost of increased computational complexity. Semi-implicit methods strike a balance between the two, providing stability with moderate computational overhead. The choice of integration method can influence the effectiveness of adaptive time stepping, and developers must carefully evaluate the trade-offs to achieve optimal performance.

In addition to error estimates and integration methods, other factors can influence the time step size in adaptive time stepping. These factors include the physical properties of the simulated objects, such as mass, stiffness, and damping, as well as the nature of the interactions between objects. For example, simulations involving soft bodies or deformable materials may require smaller time steps to accurately capture the complex behavior of the materials. Similarly, interactions involving high-speed impacts or sudden forces may necessitate smaller time steps to ensure stability and accuracy. By considering these factors, developers can fine-tune the adaptive time-stepping algorithm to suit the specific requirements of their simulations.

Implementing adaptive time stepping also involves managing the computational overhead associated with dynamically adjusting the time step size. Frequent adjustments to the time step size can introduce additional computational costs, potentially offsetting the performance gains. To mitigate this overhead, developers can employ strategies such as time step prediction and interpolation. Time step prediction involves estimating the optimal time step size based on the simulation's current state and anticipated future behavior. By predicting the time step size in advance, the simulation can reduce the frequency of adjustments and improve overall efficiency. Interpolation techniques, on the other hand, allow the simulation to transition smoothly between different time step sizes, minimizing the impact of abrupt changes and maintaining stability.

Another practical aspect of adaptive time stepping is its integration with existing game engine frameworks. Many modern game engines provide built-in support for time-stepping methods, including fixed and adaptive time stepping. Leveraging these built-in features can streamline the implementation process and ensure compatibility with other components of the game engine. Additionally, developers can extend the functionality of existing frameworks by incorporating custom adaptive time-stepping algorithms tailored to their specific simulation requirements. This flexibility allows developers to harness the benefits of adaptive time stepping while maintaining seamless integration with the broader game engine architecture.

The effectiveness of adaptive time stepping can be further enhanced through continuous monitoring and refinement. As the simulation progresses, developers can collect performance metrics and error data to evaluate the impact of the adaptive time-stepping algorithm. By analyzing this data, developers can identify areas for improvement and fine-tune the algorithm to achieve better performance and accuracy. Iterative refinement ensures that the adaptive time-stepping mechanism evolves in response to the simulation's changing dynamics, leading to continuous optimization and improved simulation quality.

To finalize, adaptive time stepping offers a powerful technique for enhancing the performance of physics simulations in game engines. By dynamically adjusting the time step size based on the simulation's current state, developers can achieve a balance between accuracy and computational efficiency. The principles and strategies discussed in this section provide a comprehensive framework for implementing adaptive time stepping, enabling developers to optimize their simulations and deliver a more immersive and responsive gaming experience. As game worlds continue to grow in complexity, adaptive time stepping will remain a valuable tool in the pursuit of realistic and high-performance physics simulations.

Level of Detail (LOD) Approaches in Physics Simulations

In game development, the quest for realism often comes with the challenge of balancing visual fidelity and computational efficiency. One of the pivotal strategies employed to achieve this balance is the Level of Detail (LOD) technique. While LOD is traditionally associated with graphical rendering, its application in physics simulations offers significant performance gains. This section explores the principles, benefits, and implementation strategies of LOD in physics simulations, providing developers with practical insights to optimize their game engines.

At its core, the concept of LOD involves varying the complexity of a simulation based on certain criteria, such as the distance from the camera or the importance of the object in the game scenario. By adjusting the level of detail, developers can allocate computational resources more efficiently, ensuring that high-fidelity simulations are reserved for critical interactions while less crucial elements are simplified.

One of the primary advantages of LOD in physics simulations is the reduction of computational load. In a typical game environment, not all objects require detailed physical interactions at all times. For instance, objects that are far from the player's viewpoint or those that have minimal impact on gameplay can be simulated with lower fidelity. By simplifying the physics calculations for these objects, developers can free up computational resources, which can then be redirected to more critical elements of the simulation.

Implementing LOD in physics simulations requires a careful consideration of various factors, including the criteria for switching between different levels of detail and the methods for simplifying the physics models. One common approach is distance-based LOD, where the complexity of the simulation decreases with increasing distance from the camera. For example, objects that are close to the player may use a detailed physics model with accurate collision detection and response, while distant objects may use a simplified model with basic collision approximations.

Another approach to LOD in physics simulations is importance-based LOD, where the level of detail is determined by the significance of the object in the game scenario. Objects that play a crucial role in gameplay, such as interactive items or key environmental features, are simulated with high fidelity. In contrast, background elements or objects with negligible impact on gameplay can be simplified. This approach ensures that the most important aspects of the game receive the necessary computational resources, enhancing the overall player experience.

The process of simplifying physics models for LOD can take various forms, depending on the nature of the simulation and the desired level of detail. One common technique is geometric simplification, where the complexity of the object's geometry is reduced. For instance, a detailed mesh collider can be replaced with a simpler bounding box or sphere collider for distant objects. This reduction in geometric complexity not only decreases the computational load but also speeds up collision detection processes.

Another technique for simplifying physics models is the approximation of physical properties. For example, complex materials with intricate deformation behaviors can be approximated with simpler materials that exhibit basic elastic properties. This approximation reduces the computational overhead associated with simulating detailed material interactions, while still providing a reasonable representation of the object's physical behavior.

Dynamic LOD is another approach that can be employed in physics simulations. Unlike static LOD, where the level of detail is determined at the start of the simulation, dynamic LOD adjusts the detail level in real-time based on the simulation's evolving conditions. This approach allows for more flexible and responsive allocation of computational resources, ensuring that high-fidelity simulations are applied where needed most. For instance, during a high-speed chase sequence, the physics simulation for the vehicles involved can be dynamically enhanced, while the surrounding environment is simplified.

The implementation of LOD in physics simulations also involves managing the transitions between different levels of detail. Abrupt changes in the level of detail can lead to noticeable artifacts and inconsistencies in the simulation. To mitigate this, developers can use techniques such as interpolation and blending to smooth the transitions. Interpolation involves gradually adjusting the physics parameters as the object moves between different LOD levels, ensuring a seamless transition. Blending, on the other hand, combines the properties of different LOD levels to create a smooth and continuous simulation.

The effectiveness of LOD in physics simulations can be further enhanced through continuous monitoring and optimization. As the game progresses, developers can collect performance metrics and analyze the impact of LOD on the simulation. By fine-tuning the criteria for switching between LOD levels and adjusting the simplification techniques, developers can achieve a more efficient and balanced simulation. This iterative approach ensures that the LOD mechanism evolves in response to the game's dynamic conditions, leading to continuous improvement in performance and fidelity.

In addition to improving performance, LOD in physics simulations also contributes to a more immersive gaming experience. By allocating computational resources more effectively, developers can enhance the realism and responsiveness of critical interactions, such as character movements, object collisions, and environmental interactions. This enhanced realism not only improves the visual fidelity of the game but also creates a more engaging and believable game world.

The integration of LOD in physics simulations also offers scalability benefits. As games are developed for a wide range of hardware configurations, from high-end gaming PCs to mobile devices, LOD provides a mechanism to adjust the simulation's complexity based on the available computational resources. This scalability ensures that the game can deliver a consistent and enjoyable experience across different platforms, catering to a broader audience.

Moreover, LOD in physics simulations can be combined with other optimization techniques to achieve even greater performance gains. For instance, developers can use LOD in conjunction with parallel processing and multithreading to distribute the computational load more effectively. By leveraging the strengths of multiple optimization strategies, developers can create highly efficient and responsive physics simulations that meet the demands of modern game development.

In conclusion, Level of Detail (LOD) approaches in physics simulations offer a powerful tool for enhancing performance and efficiency in game engines. By varying the complexity of the simulation based on distance, importance, and dynamic conditions, developers can allocate computational resources more effectively, ensuring that high-fidelity simulations are reserved for critical interactions. The principles and strategies discussed in this section provide a comprehensive framework for implementing LOD in physics simulations, enabling developers to optimize their game engines and deliver a more immersive and responsive gaming experience. As game worlds continue to grow in complexity, LOD will remain a valuable technique in the pursuit of realistic and high-performance physics simulations.

Efficient Use of Spatial Partitioning Techniques

In game development, creating expansive and interactive environments presents unique challenges for physics simulations. The sheer volume of objects and interactions inside these environments can place a significant computational burden on game engines. One effective strategy to mitigate this issue is the use of spatial partitioning techniques. These techniques help organize and manage the simulation space, allowing for more efficient processing and resource allocation. This section delves into the principles, advantages, and implementation strategies of spatial partitioning, providing developers with practical insights to enhance the performance of their physics simulations.

Spatial partitioning involves dividing the simulation space into smaller, manageable regions, each of which can be processed independently. This division enables the game engine to focus computational resources on relevant areas, reducing the number of unnecessary calculations and improving overall efficiency. Several spatial partitioning methods can be employed, each with its unique strengths and applications.

One widely used spatial partitioning technique is the grid-based method. In this approach, the simulation space is divided into a uniform grid of cells, and each object is assigned to one or more cells based on its position. Grid-based partitioning is particularly effective for simulations with evenly distributed objects and interactions. By limiting the scope of collision detection and other calculations to objects inside the same or neighboring cells, developers can significantly reduce the computational load. However, this method may become less efficient in scenarios with highly dynamic or unevenly distributed objects, as the grid may require frequent updates or adjustments.

Another common spatial partitioning technique is the use of hierarchical data structures, such as quadtrees and octrees. Quadtrees are used for two-dimensional spaces, while octrees are suitable for three-dimensional environments. These data structures recursively divide the simulation space into smaller regions, creating a tree-like hierarchy of nodes. Each node represents a specific region and contains references to its child nodes, which represent further subdivisions. Hierarchical partitioning is particularly advantageous for simulations with varying levels of detail, as it allows for efficient querying and traversal of the simulation space. By focusing calculations on relevant nodes and their children, developers can achieve significant performance gains.

Bounding volume hierarchies (BVH) represent another effective spatial partitioning technique. BVHs use a tree structure similar to quadtrees and octrees but focus on bounding volumes that encapsulate groups of objects. Common bounding volumes include axis-aligned bounding boxes (AABB) and bounding spheres. BVHs are particularly useful for collision detection, as they allow for efficient pruning of the search space. By testing collisions between bounding volumes before considering individual objects, developers can quickly eliminate large numbers of non-colliding objects from further calculations.

Spatial hashing is another technique that can enhance the performance of physics simulations. In spatial hashing, the simulation space is divided into a grid, and each cell is assigned a unique hash value. Objects are then mapped to these hash values based on their positions. This approach allows for efficient indexing and retrieval of objects inside specific regions, reducing the computational overhead associated with collision detection and other spatial queries. Spatial hashing is particularly effective for dynamic simulations with frequent object movements, as it provides a flexible and scalable solution for managing the simulation space.

Implementing spatial partitioning techniques requires careful consideration of various factors, including the size and shape of the partitions, the distribution of objects, and the nature of the interactions. For instance, the choice of partition size can significantly impact the efficiency of the simulation. Smaller partitions may lead to more precise calculations but can increase the overhead associated with managing and updating the partitions. Conversely, larger partitions may reduce overhead but can result in less accurate simulations. Developers must strike a balance between precision and efficiency to achieve optimal performance.

Another critical aspect of spatial partitioning is the management of dynamic objects. In many simulations, objects move and interact in unpredictable ways, requiring frequent updates to the partitioning structure. Efficiently handling these updates is crucial for maintaining the performance gains achieved through spatial partitioning. Techniques such as lazy updates, where partitions are only updated when necessary, and incremental updates, where only affected regions are modified, can help manage the dynamic nature of the simulation space.

Load balancing is also an essential consideration when implementing spatial partitioning techniques. In a parallel processing environment, the workload must be evenly distributed across processing units to avoid bottlenecks and ensure optimal performance. Dynamic load balancing strategies, such as work stealing and task migration, can be employed to redistribute tasks among processing units based on their current workload. By ensuring that each processing unit is utilized efficiently, developers can maximize the performance benefits of spatial partitioning.

In addition to enhancing performance, spatial partitioning techniques can also contribute to the scalability of physics simulations. As game worlds become more complex and detailed, the ability to efficiently manage and process large volumes of objects and interactions becomes increasingly important. Spatial partitioning provides a scalable solution that can adapt to the growing demands of modern game development. By organizing the simulation space into manageable regions, developers can ensure that their simulations remain responsive and efficient, even as the complexity of the game world increases.

The integration of spatial partitioning techniques with other optimization strategies can further enhance the performance of physics simulations. For instance, combining spatial partitioning with parallel processing and multithreading can distribute the computational load more effectively, allowing for simultaneous processing of independent regions. Similarly, integrating spatial partitioning with level of detail (LOD) techniques can allocate computational resources more efficiently, ensuring that high-fidelity simulations are reserved for critical interactions while less important elements are simplified.

Continuous monitoring and refinement of spatial partitioning techniques are essential for maintaining and improving the performance of physics simulations. As the simulation progresses, developers can collect performance metrics and analyze the impact of spatial partitioning on the simulation. By fine-tuning the partitioning parameters and adjusting the partitioning strategy based on the simulation's evolving conditions, developers can achieve a more efficient and balanced simulation. This iterative approach ensures that the spatial partitioning mechanism evolves in response to the game's dynamic conditions, leading to continuous optimization and improved simulation quality.

In conclusion, spatial partitioning techniques offer a powerful tool for enhancing the performance of physics simulations in game engines. By dividing the simulation space into smaller, manageable regions, developers can focus computational resources on relevant areas, reducing unnecessary calculations and improving overall efficiency. The principles and strategies discussed in this section provide a comprehensive framework for implementing spatial partitioning, enabling developers to optimize their simulations and deliver a more immersive and responsive gaming experience. As game worlds continue to grow in complexity, spatial partitioning will remain a valuable technique in the pursuit of realistic and high-performance physics simulations.

Reducing Computational Overhead with Approximation Methods

In the intricate world of game development, achieving high-performance physics simulations often entails navigating the delicate balance between computational efficiency and realistic behavior. One effective way to address this challenge is through the use of approximation methods. These techniques allow developers to simplify complex calculations, thereby reducing the computational load without significantly compromising the accuracy of the simulation. This section explores various approximation methods and their applications, providing developers with practical insights to enhance the performance of their physics simulations.

Approximation methods are fundamentally about making informed trade-offs. By approximating certain aspects of the simulation, developers can achieve considerable performance gains, making it feasible to run complex simulations in real-time. These methods are particularly useful in scenarios where precise calculations are either computationally prohibitive or unnecessary for achieving the desired level of realism.

One widely used approximation technique is the simplification of collision detection. In a typical physics simulation, collision detection can be one of the most computationally intensive tasks, especially when dealing with a large number of objects. To mitigate this, developers can use simplified collision models, such as bounding boxes or spheres, instead of detailed mesh colliders. Bounding boxes, for instance, are rectangular volumes that encapsulate an object, providing a quick way to check for potential collisions. While this method may not capture the exact shape of the object, it significantly reduces the number of calculations required, thereby enhancing performance.

Another effective approximation method involves the use of reduced-order models. These models simplify the physics equations governing the behavior of objects by focusing on the most critical aspects of the simulation. For example, in fluid dynamics simulations, developers can use the shallow water equations instead of the full Navier-Stokes equations to approximate the behavior of water surfaces. This approach provides a reasonable balance between accuracy and computational efficiency, making it suitable for real-time applications.

In addition to collision detection and reduced-order models, developers can employ approximation methods to simplify the representation of physical properties. For instance, instead of simulating the detailed deformation behavior of a soft body, developers can use a simplified spring-mass model. This model represents the object as a network of interconnected springs and masses, which can approximate the overall deformation behavior without requiring complex calculations. By using such simplified models, developers can achieve real-time performance while still providing a believable representation of the object's physical behavior.

Another area where approximation methods can be highly effective is in the simulation of rigid body dynamics. In many cases, the exact calculation of forces and torques acting on a rigid body can be computationally expensive. To address this, developers can use impulse-based methods, which approximate the effects of forces by applying instantaneous changes in velocity. This approach simplifies the calculations and allows for efficient simulation of rigid body interactions, such as collisions and joint constraints.

Furthermore, approximation methods can be applied to the simulation of large-scale environments. In scenarios where the simulation involves a vast number of objects, such as in open-world games, developers can use techniques like level-of-detail (LOD) and culling to reduce the computational burden. LOD involves varying the complexity of the simulation based on the object's importance or distance from the camera, while culling eliminates objects that are not visible or relevant to the current scene. By combining these techniques with approximation methods, developers can manage the computational load effectively, ensuring smooth and responsive simulations.

One of the key considerations when using approximation methods is the trade-off between accuracy and performance. While these techniques can significantly enhance performance, they may introduce some level of error or artifacts into the simulation. To mitigate this, developers can use adaptive methods that dynamically adjust the level of approximation based on the simulation's requirements. For example, in a physics simulation involving a character interacting with the environment, the approximation level can be reduced when the character is in close proximity to objects, ensuring accurate interactions, while a higher level of approximation can be used for distant objects.

Implementing approximation methods also requires careful attention to the specific requirements of the simulation. Different types of simulations may benefit from different approximation techniques, and developers must evaluate the trade-offs based on the desired level of realism and performance. For instance, in a racing game, the approximation of tire friction and suspension dynamics can significantly impact the gameplay experience, and developers must choose techniques that provide a good balance between accuracy and computational efficiency.

Another practical aspect of using approximation methods is the integration with existing game engine frameworks. Many modern game engines provide built-in support for various approximation techniques, such as simplified collision models and reduced-order physics equations. Leveraging these built-in features can streamline the implementation process and ensure compatibility with other components of the game engine. Additionally, developers can extend the functionality of existing frameworks by incorporating custom approximation algorithms tailored to their specific simulation requirements.

The effectiveness of approximation methods can be further enhanced through continuous monitoring and refinement. As the simulation progresses, developers can collect performance metrics and error data to evaluate the impact of the approximation techniques. By analyzing this data, developers can identify areas for improvement and fine-tune the algorithms to achieve better performance and accuracy. Iterative refinement ensures that the approximation methods evolve in response to the simulation's changing dynamics, leading to continuous optimization and improved simulation quality.

In summary, approximation methods offer a powerful tool for reducing computational overhead in physics simulations. By simplifying complex calculations and making informed trade-offs, developers can achieve significant performance gains while maintaining a reasonable level of accuracy. The principles and strategies discussed in this section provide a comprehensive framework for implementing approximation methods, enabling developers to optimize their simulations and deliver a more immersive and responsive gaming experience. As game worlds continue to grow in complexity, approximation methods will remain a valuable technique in the pursuit of realistic and high-performance physics simulations.

www.ingramcontent.com/pod-product-compliance
Lightning Source LLC
Chambersburg PA
CBHW062312220526
45479CB00004B/1144